GREAT SPOIL

GREAT SPOIL

Thomas Manton's Spirituality of the Word

J. Stephen Yuille

Reformation Heritage Books
Grand Rapids, Michigan

Great Spoil
© 2019 by J. Stephen Yuille

Reformation Heritage Books
2965 Leonard St. NE
Grand Rapids, MI 49525
616-977-0889
orders@heritagebooks.org
www.heritagebooks.org

Printed in the United States of America
19 20 21 22 23 24/10 9 8 7 6 5 4 3 2 1

Library of Congress Cataloging-in-Publication Data

Names: Yuille, J. Stephen, 1968- author.
Title: Great spoil : Thomas Manton's spirituality of the word / J. Stephen Yuille.
Description: Grand Rapids, Michigan : Reformation Heritage Books, 2019. |
    Includes bibliographical references.
Identifiers: LCCN 2019019295 (print) | LCCN 2019021937 (ebook) | ISBN
    9781601786920 (epub) | ISBN 9781601786913 (pbk. : alk. paper)
Subjects: LCSH: Manton, Thomas, 1620-1677. | Bible. Psalms, CXIX—Sermons—
    Criticism, interpretation, etc.
Classification: LCC BS1450 119th (ebook) | LCC BS1450 119th .Y848 2019 (print) |
    DDC 223/.206—dc23
LC record available at https://lccn.loc.gov/2019019295

For additional Reformed literature, request a free book list from Reformation Heritage Books at the above regular or e-mail address.

In memory of a dear mother, mother-in-law, and nana
Irene Laura Richardson (née McIntosh)
1931–2018

Table of Contents

Introduction

What is Puritanism? The term has been used to describe Thomas Cartwright, William Perkins, John Preston, John Goodwin, John Bunyan, John Milton, Oliver Cromwell, John Owen, Richard Baxter, John Cotton, Jonathan Edwards, and countless others, yet it is impossible to define *Puritanism* in a manner that encompasses all these men. Richard Greaves attributes the confusion surrounding the term to its "multiplicity of meanings" in the Elizabethan and Jacobean era.[1] At that time it was widely employed in a derogatory fashion to disparage one's opponents. Given its somewhat promiscuous usage, it is ill-advised to speak of Puritanism without first establishing what one means by the term. Heeding my own advice, I begin with a definition.

During the reign of Bloody Mary (r. 1553–1558), many Protestants suffered a grisly death at the stake. Many more escaped the queen's ferocity by fleeing to the Continent, and in 1554 most of these exiles settled in Frankfurt, where they quickly summoned John Knox from Geneva to serve as their pastor. Under Knox's oversight, they adopted a modified version of the Prayer Book, which had been produced during the reign of Edward VI (r. 1547–1553). It notably abolished any practice deemed contrary to the Reformed faith. The following year, in 1555, a new wave of English exiles arrived, led by Richard Cox, vice-chancellor of Oxford. Soon after their arrival, they made it known to their fellow

---

1. Richard Greaves, "The Puritan-Nonconformist Tradition in England, 1560–1700: Historiographical Reflections," *Albion* XVII (1985): 449.

countrymen that they desired "the face of an English church."[2] They favored the Prayer Book in its original form and desired to work within the established church as it was. From that moment, the congregation was divided between the supporters of Knox and Cox. Although united in their opposition to Mary and Roman Catholicism, these two factions did not share a common view on the nature or extent of the Reformation in England, nor did they agree as to the final authority in the ordering of public worship; Cox supporters appealed to the Prayer Book, whereas Knox supporters appealed to Scripture. Before long, the Cox faction gained control of the church, forcing Knox (and many of his followers) to depart for Geneva.

This sharp disagreement was a harbinger of things to come within the Church of England. When Mary died in 1558, Elizabeth I became the new monarch, and the Frankfurt division soon took center stage. Given England's precarious political condition, Elizabeth's ministers called for moderation. She heeded their advice, as she was well aware of the various factions within the established church. She implemented what is known as the Elizabethan Settlement, which rested on two acts of Parliament in 1559. The first, the Act of Supremacy, restored the preeminence of the Church of England to the monarch, while the second, the Act of Uniformity, enforced a new Prayer Book—a slight revision of Edward VI's edition. These acts were designed to find a via media (middle way) between the splintered groups. The form of church worship and government remained intact, and the clergy continued to dress in their traditional habits; however, the Elizabethan Settlement called for the abolishment of prayers to the saints and the removal of relics and images from churches. Most significantly, it engineered the dismissal of the fourteen surviving bishops from Mary's reign. Four years later, in 1563, the Church of England established the Thirty-Nine Articles of Religion,[3] which clearly placed it within the framework of ancient councils and historic creeds. These articles also espoused the

2. As quoted by William M'Gavin, "Life of John Knox," in John Knox, *The History of the Reformation of Religion in Scotland* (Glasgow: Blackie, Fullarton, & Co., 1831), xxxvii.

3. Parliament officially authorized these eight years later.

teaching of the Reformation on Scripture, free will, justification, and good works while also openly opposing Roman Catholic dogmas such as purgatory and transubstantiation, and practices such as invoking the saints and adoring the Eucharist.

Not everyone was thrilled with the Elizabethan Settlement. As expected, Roman Catholics lamented the reversal of Mary's policies, but Protestants were also deeply divided over the implemented changes, mirroring the old Frankfurt debate. Some were satisfied with the Elizabethan Settlement, whereas others longed for greater reform. Among the latter were many who wanted to remove all perceived remnants of Roman Catholicism. Some of them also desired to alter the church's government on the basis of Presbyterianism. These men encompassed a broad spectrum of opinion, yet all shared one common denominator—dissatisfaction with the extent of the English Reformation. As one historian notes, "The term 'Puritan' became current during the 1560s as a nickname for Protestants who, dissatisfied with the Elizabethan Settlement of the church…would have subscribed to the contention of the Admonition to Parliament of 1572 that 'we in England are so far off, from having a church rightly reformed, according to the prescript of God's Word, that as yet we are not come to the outward face of the same.'"[4]

While varied in their aim and intensity, the Puritans' struggle for ecclesiastical change continued through the reigns of the Stuart kings, until the Great Ejection of 1662 when Charles II (r. 1660–1685) introduced an Act of Uniformity, effectively forcing close to two thousand ministers out of the established church and into dissent.

During this one-hundred-year period (1558–1662), the term *Puritan* assumed an additional meaning to the one described above. At the end of the sixteenth century, William Perkins lamented, "Who are so much branded with vile terms of Puritans and Precisians, as those that most endeavour to get and keep the purity of heart in a

---

4. Neil Keeble, "Puritan Spirituality," in *The Westminster Dictionary of Christian Spirituality*, ed. G. S. Wakefield (Philadelphia: Westminster Press, 1983), 323.

good conscience?"[5] Writing in 1611, Robert Bolton commented, "The world is come to that wretched pass, and height of profaneness, that even honesty and sanctification is many times odiously branded by the nick-name Puritanism."[6] In 1641, Thomas Wilson noted that "fervency in religion" is called "indiscretion, rashness, puritanism, or headiness."[7] It is evident that, in addition to its political and ecclesiastical usage, the term *Puritan* became a derogatory moniker for those who practiced a certain style of piety—what we might call "experimental Calvinism"—which transcended the deep divisions between those of differing political and ecclesiastical views: Independents and Presbyterians, Parliamentarians and Royalists, conformists and nonconformists, credobaptists and paedobaptists.[8] At its center stood the conviction that believers must experience an affective appropriation of God's sovereign grace, moving beyond intellectual assent to heartfelt dedication to Christ. These Puritans preached with great enthusiasm about God's sovereign grace from eternity, but they were particularly concerned about how this grace breaks through in time into the believer's experience. They wanted to explain how believers respond to God's sovereign acts—that is, how the covenant of grace impacts them and moves them from initial faith to full assurance.

Central to this experimental Calvinism was the Bible. The Puritans were convinced that the Spirit of God works in His people through His Word.[9] William Perkins, for example, affirmed that "the holy use of

---

5. William Perkins, *A Godly and Learned Exposition upon Christ's Sermon in the Mount*, in *The Works of William Perkins* (London, 1631), 3:15.

6. Robert Bolton, *A Discourse about the State of True Happiness: Delivered in Certain Sermons in Oxford, and at Paul's Cross* (London, 1611), 132.

7. Thomas Wilson, *David's Zeal for Zion: A Sermon Preached before the Honourable House of Commons, April 4, 1641* (London, 1641), 14.

8. For more on these definitions, see J. Stephen Yuille, *Puritan Spirituality: The Fear of God in the Affective Theology of George Swinnock* (Milton Keynes, UK: Paternoster, 2007), 5–17.

9. This conviction was central to the Reformation, which involved a major shift of emphasis in the cultivation of Christian spirituality. Roman Catholicism had majored on symbols and images as the means of cultivating spirituality. The Reformers, however, turned to words—both spoken and written. They championed a thoroughly "biblical" spirituality.

the Word" is the means "whereby we draw near unto heaven itself."[10] According to Perkins, the Holy Spirit unites the heavenly and the creaturely in a *sacramental* union, producing spiritual effects (faith) through physical means (the reading, hearing, and preaching of God's Word). As the Father gave the Son objectively in history, He now gives the Son objectively through His Word. The issue is not divine presence, but divine action. For Perkins (and those who stand in the same tradition) the implication is that if we absent ourselves from the Word, we isolate ourselves from Christ and remove ourselves from His kingdom.[11] On this basis, the Puritans argued for the sole sufficiency of Scripture; that is to say, they affirmed that the nature of the Holy Spirit's work in the authors of Scripture was unique and that the Holy Spirit now *illumines* what He then *inspired*.

The Puritans defended their position against the Roman Catholics, who championed church tradition as revelation.[12] They were also forced to defend their position against the Anabaptists (and, later, the Quakers), who urged people to turn to the "inner light" to hear God's voice. For these "radicals," the indwelling Holy Spirit is more powerful than the words of Scripture. They maintained that the Bible is indeed precious but that the indwelling Holy Spirit is the supreme authority when it comes to direction for Christian living and thinking.[13] The Puritans viewed this "anabaptistical" position as dangerous because it made an unwarranted cleavage between the Spirit and the Word.[14]

---

10. William Perkins, *A Godly and Learned Exposition upon the Whole Epistle of Jude* (London: Felix Kingston, 1606), 64.

11. Perkins, *Jude*, 122.

12. The Roman Catholic view crystallized between the years 1100 and 1400. Simply put, Scripture and Tradition are two distinct sources of divine revelation; therefore, both constitute the inspired Word of God. According to the Council of Trent (1546), "Saving truth and rules of conduct" are "contained in the written books and in the unwritten traditions, which, received by the apostles from the mouth of Christ Himself, or from the apostles themselves, the Holy Ghost dictating, have come down to us.... God is the author of both" (Session 4).

13. By way of example, see Isaac Penington, *Letters of Isaac Penington*, 2nd ed. (London: Holdsworth and Ball, 1829), 202–3.

14. The Puritans stood in the tradition of the Reformers, who opposed the radicals on account of their exaltation of personal interpretation over corporate interpretation as

The Puritan position on the sufficiency of Scripture received creedal sanction in 1646 with the publication of the Westminster Confession of Faith, which states, "The whole counsel of God...is either expressly set down in Scripture, or by good and necessary consequence may be deduced from Scripture: unto which nothing at any time is to be added, whether by new revelations of the Spirit [i.e., the Radicals, Anabaptists, Quakers, etc.], or traditions of men [i.e., the Roman Catholics]."[15] According to the confession, the Bible is the only deposit of divine revelation and therefore is the meeting place between Christ and believers. Again, it is the instrument through which the Spirit of God works in the people of God.

In contrast to the Puritan commitment to the sufficiency of Scripture, mysticism is rooted in the conviction that we can attain an immediate knowledge of God and His will through personal experience as we listen for His voice in our hearts—a voice we discern in "gusts of emotion" and "inner urgings."[16] Regrettably, many today

---

well as their expectation of new revelation. The radicals did not stress how God comes to us (i.e., through the Word and sacraments) but rather how we come to God. In sharp contrast, the Reformers affirmed that God gives the Word as the means by which He gives the Spirit. Richard Lovelace summarizes as follows: "In order to guard against the prophetic pretensions of enthusiasts and the Roman Catholic appeal to the guidance of the Spirit in her Magisterium, the Reformers and the Puritans strongly guarded their doctrine of the Holy Spirit by a stress on the objectivity of the written Word. In the Reformed tradition, revelation was confined to Scripture, although it was acknowledged that illumination by the Holy Spirit was necessary for the understanding and application of the Word." *Dynamics of Spiritual Life: An Evangelical Theology of Renewal* (Downers Grove, Ill.: IVP Academic, 1979), 263.

15. WCF 1.6. See also the London Baptist Confession of 1689, 1.6. Interestingly, it includes a sentence to its description of Holy Scripture that is not found in the WCF: "The Holy Scripture is the all-sufficient, certain and infallible rule or standard of the knowledge, faith and obedience that constitute salvation" (1.1). Three qualifiers are added to the expression *rule or standard* to make the point that there is no authority apart from Scripture. Nothing is to be added—whether by oral tradition (Roman Catholics) or new revelation (Quakers). This addition was likely the result of the growing concern among Particular Baptists over the number of Quakers interacting with Baptist churches.

16. J. I. Packer and Carolyn Nystrom, *Guard Us, Guide Us: Divine Leading in Life's Decisions* (Grand Rapids: Baker Books, 2008), 14. But how are we to understand our "inner urgings"? According to John Murray, we will experience feelings, impressions,

believe they are able to sense the Holy Spirit working directly (apart from the Bible) within them, producing impulses and intuitions as a means of communicating His will to them. In so doing, they have made their relationship with God contingent on nebulous feelings. Even more troubling is the fact that they have severed the Spirit of God from the Word of God, thereby divorcing Him from the only infallible and sufficient revelation that He has given us—namely, the Bible.

It seems that far too many Evangelicals have forsaken the Word-based piety that their Puritan forefathers worked so hard to define and defend. That being the case, my goal in this book is to redirect us back to a model of biblical piety (or, spirituality) through an examination of Thomas Manton's sermons on Psalm 119. After a brief acquaintance with Manton as a leading Puritan committed to the ministry of the Word (chapter 2), I investigate the concept of blessedness so foundational to his piety (chapters 3–9). In sum, he believes that God impresses His excellencies on us through His Word, thereby stirring our affections so that we make returns to Him—namely, faith, love, humility, and repentance. God's Word, therefore, is the instrument by which God speaks to us and we respond to Him (chapters 10–14). Given the fact that the Spirit of God works only through the Word of God, Manton is convinced that we should devote ourselves to it through the practice of spiritual duties (chapters 15–21).

This is how Manton understands the blessed man's pursuit in Psalm 119, and it is this emphasis that invariably shapes his biblical piety. At the foundation stands the conviction that as we love and obey God's Word, the blessed God communes with us by His Spirit, conveying sweet influences on our soul through His Word. Thus, we expect God

---

convictions, and so on as we respond to the Holy Spirit's work of illumination "through the Word of God." But this is not to be confused with the mystic's belief that the state of our consciousness (i.e., feelings) is the result of a "direct intimation" of the Holy Spirit's will to us. See John Murray, "The Guidance of the Holy Spirit," in Sinclair B. Ferguson, *From the Mouth of God: Trusting, Reading, and Applying the Bible* (Edinburgh: Banner of Truth, 2014), 185. By and large, modern evangelicalism has abandoned the Puritans' emphasis on the spirituality of the Word, choosing instead to follow the path of the Anabaptists and Quakers. This trend is so widespread that a subtle mysticism has become the presumptive position among most evangelicals.

to speak to us—not subjectively through inner urgings, but through His Word. The Bible is God's voice—that which "goeth forth out of [God's] mouth" (Isa. 55:11). It bridges the expanse between heaven and earth, Creator and creature. It is as powerful as the rain and snow that cometh down from heaven and "returneth not thither, but watereth the earth, and maketh it bring forth and bud, that it may give seed to the sower, and bread to the eater" (Isa. 55:10). For this reason, we listen to the Bible as if we heard God speaking to us from heaven, rejoicing like those who find "great spoil" (Ps. 119:162).

Chapter 1

Thomas Manton

Thomas Manton was born at Lydeard St. Lawrence, Somerset, on March 31, 1620.[1] After completing grammar school, he enrolled at Wadham College, Oxford, and graduated four years later with a bachelor of arts. Since advanced degrees did not require his presence at Oxford, he would go on to complete the bachelor of divinity in 1654 and the doctor of divinity in 1660 while engaged in ministry.

Upon his ordination to the diaconate in 1639, Manton embarked on his first lectureship at the parish church of Culliton (Colyton),

---

1. The standard account of Manton's life is William Harris, "Some Memoirs of the Life and Character of the Reverend and Learned Thomas Manton, D. D.," in Thomas Manton, *The Complete Works of Thomas Manton* (1870–1875; repr., Birmingham, Ala.: Solid Ground Christian Books, 2008), 1:vii–xxxiii. Harris's biographical sketch is based on two earlier accounts: William Bates, "A Funeral Sermon Preached upon the Death of the Reverend and Excellent Divine, Dr. Thomas Manton," in Manton, *Works*, 22:123–47; and Anthony Wood, *Athenae Oxonienses* (London, 1691), 2:446–48. Additional summaries of Manton's life are found in Edmund Calamy, *The Nonconformist's Memorial: Being an Account of the Ministers, Who Were Ejected or Silenced after the Restoration, Particularly by the Act of Uniformity, Which Took Place on Bartholomew-Day, Aug. 24, 1662* (London, 1775), 1:138–41; and Joel R. Beeke and Randall J. Pederson, *Meet the Puritans: With a Guide to Modern Reprints* (Grand Rapids: Reformation Heritage Books, 2006), 407–9. For a more thorough analysis of Manton in his historical context, see Derek Cooper, "The Ecumenical Exegete: Thomas Manton's Commentary on James in Relation to Its Protestant Predecessors, Contemporaries and Successors" (PhD thesis, Lutheran Theological Seminary, 2008); and Adam Richardson, "Thomas Manton and the Presbyterians in Interregnum and Restoration England" (PhD thesis, University of Leicester, 2014).

Devon. In order to avoid the growing political unrest in the region, he moved a short time later with his new bride, Mary Morgan, to London. In 1644, St. Mary's Church in Stoke Newington was sequestered, and the pastorate was offered to Manton. He held this position until becoming pastor of St. Paul's in Covent Garden a few years later.

These were eventful years for the nation, and Manton found himself in the midst of significant social and political upheaval. In 1641, Parliament passed the Grand Remonstrance, which eventually led to the Civil War between Parliamentarians and Royalists. After the former's victory in 1646, Charles I attempted to persuade Scotland to invade England under the promise that he would establish Presbyterianism. Disappointed by the Long Parliament's unwillingness to confront the king, Thomas Pride (a colonel in the new model army) "purged" it of close to two hundred members in 1648. The remaining members constituted the new Rump Parliament, which eventually tried and executed the king for treason. Manton played no role in this. While it is true that he served as one of the three clerks at the Westminster Assembly, penned the introduction to the assembly's documents, preached occasionally before Parliament, and prayed at various ceremonies related to Oliver Cromwell's Protectorship, Manton remained a committed royalist. He was one of fifty-seven divines who signed a protest against the Rump Parliament's plan to execute the king.

Despite his outspoken opposition to the regicide, Manton was a prominent figure during Oliver Cromwell's Protectorship. He quickly became a leading voice in political and theological matters, serving on numerous commissions. After Richard Cromwell's Protectorship failed in 1660, General Monck restored the Long Parliament by reinstating those members who had been excluded twelve years earlier. It immediately dissolved itself and convened the new Convention Parliament, composed mostly of Presbyterians favorable to the return of Charles II. Manton was very active in this endeavor. According to J. C. Ryle, "If there was one name which more than another was incessantly before the public for several years about the period of the Restoration, that name was Manton's."[2] He was even one of the delegates who met with Charles II at Breda in order to negotiate the terms of his return.

Upon his restoration, the king convened the new Cavalier Parliament, thereby sweeping away any hopes for compromise between Presbyterians and Episcopalians. It passed the Act of Uniformity in 1662, requiring all who had not received Episcopal ordination to be reordained by bishops; moreover, it required ministers to declare their consent to the entire Book of Common Prayer and their rejection of the Solemn League and Covenant. As a result, approximately two thousand ministers (including Manton) left the Church of England. While actively seeking accommodation for Presbyterians within the national church, Manton continued to preach privately. Because of his violation of the Five Mile Act, he was imprisoned for six months in 1670;[3] however, the political indulgence two years later allowed him to preach openly at his home in Covent Garden. Soon after, he became a lecturer at Pinner's Hall, where he remained in this capacity until his death on October 18, 1677.

At Manton's funeral, William Bates preached on 1 Thessalonians 4:17, "And so shall we ever be with the Lord."[4] In the course of his sermon, he praised his close friend for "the holiness of his person," extolling in particular his constancy, loyalty, charity, and humility.[5] Bates also praised Manton for "the quality of his office," affirming that he possessed "a clear judgment, rich fancy, strong memory, and happy elocution."[6] These characteristics, coupled with his extraordinary knowledge of Scripture, made him an excellent minister of the gospel. According to Bates, the goal of Manton's preaching was to open eyes so that people might see "their wretched condition as sinners"; to cause them to flee "from the wrath to come"; to make them "humbly,

2. J. C. Ryle, "An Estimate of Manton," in Manton, *Works*, 2:vii.

3. This act prohibited ministers from coming within five miles of the parish church from which they had been ejected.

4. Bates, "Funeral Sermon," in Manton, *Works*, 22:123–47. J. C. Ryle provides an insightful assessment of Manton as a man, writer, theologian, and expositor. See his "Estimate of Manton," 2:iii–xiii.

5. Bates, "Funeral Sermon," 22:146.

6. Bates, "Funeral Sermon," 22:143.

thankfully and entirely" receive Christ as their all-sufficient Savior;
and to edify them "in their most holy faith."[7] The style of Manton's
preaching was commensurate with his goal. "His expression," writes
Bates, "was natural and free, clear and eloquent, quick and powerful…
this man of God was inflamed with a holy zeal, and from thence such
ardent expressions broke forth as were capable to procure attention
and consent in his hearers."[8] By all accounts, Bates's high estimation
of Manton's preaching was fully warranted.[9] According to Edmund
Calamy, Manton "left behind him the general reputation of as excellent a preacher as this city or nation hath produced."[10]

In a letter, dated August 1, 1684, included as a preface to Manton's
published sermons on Matthew 25, three ministers (William Bates,
John Collinges, and John Howe)[11] encourage the reader to seek out
sermons that are "substantial, scriptural, and practical,"[12] adding, "all
other discourses are abusively called preaching, and Athens were a
more proper place for them than a preacher's pulpit."[13] Interestingly, in
the course of their commendation of Manton for his "solid" discourses,
they provide a brief overview of the history of preaching.

---

7. Bates, "Funeral Sermon," 22:144. Manton was Reformed in his soteriology. See
Works, 3:328–31; 5:475–84; 12:295–96, 314–15; 20:326, 361. However, he modeled
his preaching on Christ, particularly His free offer of the gospel. See *Works*, 13:293. For
a brief discussion of the relationship between his soteriology and preaching, see Donald
J. MacLean, "Thomas Manton (1620–1677)," in *James Durham (1622–1658) and the
Gospel Offer in Its Seventeenth-Century Context* (Göttingen: Vandenhoeck & Ruprecht,
2015), 197–214.

8. Bates, "Funeral Sermon," 22:144–45.

9. In the opinion of Archbishop James Ussher, Manton was one of the "best
preachers in England." See Harris, "Some Memoirs," in Manton, *Works*, 1:xi.

10. Edmund Calamy, *An Abridgement of Mr. Baxter's History of His Life and Times*
(London, 1702), 210.

11. William Bates (1625–1699), John Collinges (1623–1690), and John Howe
(1630–1705) were Manton's contemporaries. Like Manton, they were Presbyterian ministers, ejected for nonconformity in 1662. Each published popular works on divinity.

12. Thomas Manton, "To the Reader," *Several Sermons upon the Twenty-Fifth
Chapter of Matthew*, in Manton, *Works*, 9:316.

13. Manton, "To the Reader," 9:316.

They begin by highlighting two famous preachers of the ancient church: Chrysostom and Augustine.[14] They applaud these two for their "judicious explications of Scripture"—for their "plenty of matter, clearness of judgment, [and] orderliness of method." Moving into the Middle Ages, the three ministers note a dramatic shift in preaching. They contend that it "turned into trifling about scholastic niceties," whereby preachers found their chief texts in John Duns Scotus (1266–1308) or Thomas Aquinas (c. 1225–1274) rather than in Scripture. The Reformation, however, marked another pivotal turning point in the history of preaching. The three ministers speak glowingly of Martin Luther, Ulrich Zwingli, John Calvin, William Farel, Pierre Viret, and Theodore Beza because of their faithful handling of Scripture in the pulpit; yet they lament the subsequent generation of preachers, who (for the most part) failed to follow the example of the magisterial reformers. Finally, after reviewing the history of preaching, the three ministers arrive at their own day, affirming that God has "reserved it for a great blessing," for it is a more fertile season of preaching than "any since that of the apostles."

How do these three ministers account for this unprecedented period of homiletic blessing? They point to one man—William Perkins, declaring that he was the first to restore preaching to "its true sense" and to teach "the true manner of it."[15] Perkins's views on preaching are set down in *The Art of Prophesying*.[16] He affirmed that when a

---

14. Manton, "To the Reader," 9:316.

15. Manton, "To the Reader," 9:316–17. The three ministers add the following remark: "The generality of good preachers have made it their business to preach Christ and the exceeding riches of his grace, and to study matter rather than words, upon Mr. Perkins's old principle *verba sequenter res*." This "old principle" seems to be taken from Cato's famous dictum *rem tene, verba sequentur*, "Grasp the subject, the words will follow." Marcus Porcius Cato (234–149 BC) was a Roman statesman, often called "Cato the Elder" to distinguish him from "Cato the Younger" (his great-grandson).

16. William Perkins, *The Art of Prophesying; or, A Treatise concerning the Sacred and Only True Manner and Method of Preaching*, vol. 2 in *The Works of William Perkins* (London, 1631). It was first published in 1592 in Latin, then translated into English in 1606. It consists of eleven chapters, covering the principles of hermeneutics, interpretation, application, and proclamation. For a thorough treatment of Perkins's treatise, see Joseph A. Pipa, "William Perkins and the Development of Puritan Preaching" (PhD

preacher stands before his congregation, he does so "in the name and room of Christ," with the goal of calling people into a state of grace and preserving them therein.[17] Preaching, therefore, is the means by which we experience God's grace from conversion to glorification.[18] It is the means by which God reveals Himself to us and imparts His grace to us. It is the instrument by which the Holy Spirit effects our union with Christ. In sum, Perkins affirms that the "only ordinary means" by which to attain faith is the Word preached. It must be "heard, remembered, practiced, and continually hid in the heart."[19] It is this conviction that led him to formulate a method of preaching that would (in his opinion) best achieve its experiential end.

---

diss., Westminster Theological Seminary, 1985). Some scholars trace Perkins's plain style of preaching to Ramism. See, for example, Donald Keith McKim, *Ramism in William Perkins's Theology* (New York: Peter Lang, 1987). Ramus (1515–1572), a convert from Roman Catholicism, proposed a method to simplify all academic subjects—a single logic for both dialectic and rhetoric. The task of the logician was to classify concepts in order to make them understandable and memorable. This was accomplished through method, or the orderly presentation of a subject. The *ars logica* quickly won the support of many Puritans, including Gabriel Harvey, a lecturer who used Ramus's method to reform the arts curriculum of grammar, rhetoric, and logic. Harvey's presentation deeply impressed Perkins, who regularly employed Ramus's method by presenting his subject's partition, often by dichotomies, into progressively more heads or topics, applying each truth set forth. Pipa demonstrates that Perkins did not slavishly follow Ramus in that he was not locked into the use of dichotomy. "William Perkins," 161–68.

17. Perkins, *Art of Prophesying*, 2:646. For a helpful discussion about urgency in Puritan preaching, see Maarten Kuivenhoven, "Condemning Coldness and Sleepy Dullness: The Concept of Urgency in the Preaching Models of Richard Baxter and William Perkins," *Puritan Reformed Journal* 4, no. 2 (July 2012): 180–200.

18. The term *experiential* (or *experimental*) comes from the Latin verb *experior* (to know by experience). Experiential preaching "addresses the vital matter of how a Christian experiences the truth of biblical, Christian doctrine in his life." Joel R. Beeke, "The Lasting Power of Reformed Experiential Preaching," in *Puritan Reformed Spirituality* (Grand Rapids: Reformation Heritage Books, 2004), 425–43.

19. William Perkins, *A Treatise Tending unto a Declaration, Whether a Man Be in the Estate of Damnation, or in the Estate of Grace: and if He Be in the First, How He May in Time Come out of It: if in the Second, How He May Discern It, and Persevere in the Same to the End*, in *Works of William Perkins* (London, 1608), 1:363.

In *The Art of Prophesying*, Perkins lays out "the sacred and only method of preaching" in four succinct steps.[20] The first is "to read the text distinctly out of the canonical Scriptures." Next is "to give the sense and understanding" of the text, which is known as interpretation: "the opening of the words and sentences of the Scripture, so that one entire and natural sense may appear."[21] The third step in preaching is "to collect a few and profitable points of doctrine," which Perkins referred to as "the right cutting of the Word."[22] In simple terms, it involves deducing the main point of a passage, both theological and practical. The final step in preaching is "to apply the doctrines rightly collected to the life and manners of men in a simple and plain speech."[23] The effectiveness of Perkins's own preaching was due in large part to this last step. He had a penchant for dealing with "cases of conscience" through careful self-examination and faithful scriptural application.[24]

Perkins recognized, however, that his experiential end (the "sense") and methodical approach (the "manner") in preaching were insufficient in themselves to effect lasting change in others. "We preachers may cry until our lungs fly out, or be spent within us, and men are moved no

---

20. For a detailed analysis, see J. Stephen Yuille, "A Simple Method: William Perkins and the Shaping of the Protestant Pulpit," *Puritan Reformed Journal* 9, no. 1 (January 2017): 215–30.

21. Perkins, *Art of Prophesying*, 2:653. Richard Muller observes that Perkins "evidences a preference for a close, literal/grammatical location of the meaning of the text coupled with, as was true of the work of his predecessors in the Reformed tradition, a strong sense of the direct theological address of the text to the church in the present." "William Perkins and the Protestant Exegetical Tradition: Interpretation, Style and Method," in *A Commentary on Hebrews 11 (1609 Edition)*, ed. John H. Augustine (New York: Pilgrim Press, 1991), 87. Muller explains Perkins's use of "scope" and "method" in exegesis—he divides each verse, explains the meaning of its parts, and then draws out the text's argument in terms of the grammatical and logical relations of the parts.

22. Perkins, *Art of Prophesying*, 2:662.

23. Perkins, *Art of Prophesying*, 2:664.

24. Ian Breward, "William Perkins and the Origins of Puritan Casuistry," *The Evangelist Quarterly* 40 (1968): 16–22; George L. Mosse, *The Holy Pretence: A Study in Christianity and Reason of State from William Perkins to John Winthrop* (Oxford: Blackwell, 1957), 48–67.

more than stones."[25] There was still a missing element—unction (the demonstration of God's power). Such power is evident when people judge that the Holy Spirit is speaking through the preacher's words and gestures. Perkins explains, "When as the minister of the Word doth in the time of preaching so behave himself, that all, even ignorant persons and unbelievers may judge, that it is not so much he that speaketh, as the Spirit of God in him and by him…. This makes the ministry to be lively and powerful."[26] But how is such unction achieved? While recognizing that anointed preaching ultimately resides in the sovereign will of the Holy Spirit, Perkins maintained that the Spirit is more likely to bless preaching marked by simplicity. Therefore, he encouraged a "plain" style because he was convinced that "a strange word hinders the understanding of those things that are spoken…. It draws the mind away from the purpose to some other matter."[27]

Manton adopted wholeheartedly Perkins's "simple" method of preaching because he believed it was the best way to convince the judgment and embrace the affections, thereby bringing the mind into vital contact with the meaning of Scripture. By all accounts, he was a skilled spiritual physician who excelled at expounding and applying God's truth to those under his pastoral care.[28]

---

25. William Perkins, *A Faithful and Plain Exposition upon the Two First Verses of the Second Chapter of Zephaniah*, in *Works of William Perkins* (London, 1631), 3:424.

26. Perkins, *Art of Prophesying*, 2:670.

27. Perkins, *Art of Prophesying*, 2:670. As Pipa observes, the "ornate" style was chiefly concerned about "the abundant use of rhetorical devices such as repetition, heaping of examples, gradation or word-chains and schemata…innumerable quotations from the church fathers and various secular sources." "Development of Puritan Preaching," 38. For more on the styles of preaching, see Perry Miller, *The New England Mind* (New York: Macmillan, 1939); J. W. Blench, *Preaching in England in the Late Fifteenth and Sixteenth Centuries* (New York: Barnes & Noble, 1964); and Horton Davies, *The Worship of English Puritans* (Morgan, Pa.: Soli Deo Gloria, 1997).

28. Manton remarks, "Were we only to provide for ourselves, we might read to you fair lectures of contemplative divinity, and with words as soft as oil entice you into a fool's paradise, never searching your wounds and sores. But our commission is to 'cry aloud, and spare not' (Isaiah 58:1)." *Exposition of James*, in Manton, *Works*, 4:436.

Over the course of his pastoral ministry, Manton preached numerous miscellaneous sermons in addition to extensive series on the Lord's Prayer, Christ's temptation, His transfiguration, Isaiah 53, 2 Thessalonians 2, Matthew 25, John 17, Romans 6 and 8, 2 Corinthians 5, Hebrews 11, Psalm 119, James, and Jude.[29] He placed such importance on preaching because he viewed it as a means of grace in which Christ was present.[30] To put it another way, he was convinced that preaching possesses "a ministerial efficacy by which the authority and sovereign efficacy of the Spirit is conveyed."[31] For this reason, he affirmed that we ought to listen to the Bible "as if we had heard [God] utter and pronounce it with his own mouth, or had received it immediately by

---

29. Manton's published works include close to one thousand sermons gathered into twenty-two volumes. Interestingly, they do not contain a single polemical or doctrinal treatise. All of his writings, therefore, are expositional. In the opinion of Hughes Oliphant Old, Manton's published works "probably give us the best sustained impression of Puritan preaching which is available." *The Reading and Preaching of the Scriptures in the Worship of the Christian Church* (Grand Rapids: Eerdmans, 2002), 4:301. For an analysis of Manton as a biblical interpreter, see Derek Cooper, *Thomas Manton: A Guided Tour of the Life and Thought of a Puritan Pastor* (Phillipsburg, N.J.: P&R Publishing, 2011), 79–142. Cooper's study focuses on Manton's sermons on the book of James.

30. Manton champions the Reformed position of *fides ex auditu*. The implication is that if we absent ourselves from preaching, we isolate ourselves from God's grace. For more on the Puritans' emphasis on the life-giving power of the Bible, see J. I. Packer, *A Quest for Godliness: The Puritan Vision of the Christian Life* (Wheaton, Ill.: Crossway, 1990), 281–84.

31. Manton, *Exposition of James*, 4:132. He would agree wholeheartedly with John Calvin's assertion (based on Rom. 10:17) that "when it pleases the Lord to work," preaching "becomes the instrument of his power." *Commentaries on the Epistle of the Apostle Paul to the Romans*, in *Calvin's Commentaries* (Grand Rapids: Baker Books, 2003), 19:401. Arnold Hunt points to two sources for the Reformed method of preaching. The first is Paul's portrayal of the inseparable link between preaching, hearing, and believing, as articulated in Romans 10:17. The second is Aristotle's theory of perception, according to which hearing contributes most to "the acquisition of knowledge." *The Art of Hearing: English Preachers and Their Audiences, 1590–1640* (Cambridge: Cambridge University Press, 2010), 22–23. For more on the relationship between the Reformed method of preaching and the Reformed doctrine of Scripture, see Mary Morrissey, "Scripture, Style, and Persuasion in Seventeenth-Century English Theories of Preaching," *Journal of Ecclesiastical History* 53, no. 4 (October 2002).

oracle from him."[32] This conviction is apparent throughout Manton's sermons, but nowhere is it more prevalent than in his 190 sermons[33] on Psalm 119.[34]

---

32. Manton, *Psalm 119*, 7:261.

33. These sermons are found in Manton, *Works*, vols. 6–9. According to Bates, Manton preached them "in his usual course of three times a week." "To the Reader," in Manton, *Works*, 6:2. In describing Manton's audience, Vincent Alsop writes, "They can here with safety read what with great danger they formerly heard." "To the Reader," in Manton, *Works*, 6:4. This remark seems to imply that Manton preached this series of sermons under some duress—perhaps in the late 1660s, after the passing of the Five Mile Act.

34. The Reformed tradition has long recognized Psalm 119 as an exemplar of biblical spirituality. Matthew Henry remarked, "Many are the instructions which we here find about a religious life. Many are the sweet experiences of one that lived such a life. Here is something or other to suit the case of every Christian." *Commentary on the Whole Bible*, ed. Leslie F. Church (Grand Rapids: Zondervan, 1961), 705. Jonathan Edwards stated that he knew of no part of Scripture "where the nature and evidences of true and sincere godliness are so fully and largely insisted on and delineated, as in the 119th Psalm." *On Religious Affections*, in *The Works of Jonathan Edwards* (1834; repr., Peabody, Mass.: Hendrickson, 1998), 1:280. William Plumer recognized one of Psalm 119's "highest excellencies" to be "its varied instruction on the nature of true, experimental religion." *Psalms: A Critical and Expository Commentary with Doctrinal and Practical Remarks* (1867; repr., Edinburgh: Banner of Truth, 1975), 1018. Similarly, Charles Bridges believed that Psalm 119 "contains the anatomy of experimental religion, the interior lineaments of the family of God. It is given for the use of believers in all ages, as an excellent touchstone of vital godliness." *Psalm 119: An Exposition* (1827; repr., Edinburgh: Banner of Truth, 1974), ix.

Chapter 2

Blessedness

Manton prefaces his sermon series on Psalm 119 by declaring that it is "a choice piece of Scripture."[1] Expectedly, he mentions that the psalm is an alphabetic acrostic poem[2] consisting of twenty-two stanzas, according to the number of letters in the Hebrew alphabet, with each

---

1. Manton, *Psalm 119*, 6:5. Manton sees little coherence in Psalm 119, commenting, "Many of the sentences have no other connection than pearls upon the same string, though some are as links in the same chain, fastened one to another by an apt method and order." *Psalm 119*, 7:95. Again, "Most of the sentences of this psalm are independent, and do not easily fall under the rules of method; so that we need not take pains in clearing up the context." *Psalm 119*, 8:420. Similarly, Matthew Henry remarks, "There is seldom any coherence between the verses, but, like Solomon's proverbs, it is a chest of gold rings, not a chain of gold links." *Commentary on the Whole Bible*, 705. Charles Bridges echoes this sentiment: "If [the verses] are not links on the same chain in continuous and unbroken dependence, they may at least be considered as pearls upon one string, of equal, though independent, value." *Psalm 119*, xi. But is this true? The psalm is a prayerful meditation, not an analytic presentation, but that is not to say it lacks coherence. In general, each stanza displays a thematic unity. The *Aleph* (1st) and *Beth* (2nd) stanzas serve as a prologue, in which the psalmist sets the foundation for the psalm by describing his relationship to "the law of the LORD." The *Gimel* (3rd) stanza marks the beginning of the prayer of lament, which continues throughout the psalm, although its emphasis varies. The *Kaph* (11th) stanza marks the pinnacle of the lament. The *Lamed* (12th) stanza notes a significant change in the psalmist's perspective and marks the psalm's zenith. The prayer of lament continues, but the psalmist's perspective (as expressed in the 12th stanza) shapes the remainder of the psalm. The *Taw* (22nd) stanza provides an appropriate conclusion: a promise of praise.

2. There are other alphabetic acrostics in the Old Testament. See Pss. 9/10, 25, 34, 37, 111, 112, 119, 145; Prov. 31:10–31; and Lam. 1–4.

stanza containing eight verses beginning with the same letter.[3] He concludes his prefatory remarks by stating his intention to devote a sermon to each verse in order.

For Manton, the first verse sets the foundation for the entire psalm: "Blessed are the undefiled in the way, who walk in the law of the LORD" (Ps. 119:1). "The Psalmist beginneth with a description of the way to true blessedness," says Manton, "as Christ began his Sermon on the Mount, and as the whole Book of Psalms is elsewhere begun. Blessedness is that which we all aim at, only we are either ignorant or reckless of the way that leadeth to it; therefore the holy Psalmist would first set us right in the true notion of a blessed man."[4] According to Manton, blessedness (or happiness) is our most fundamental pursuit: "To ask whether men would be happy or not, is to ask whether they love themselves."[5] Our problem, however, is that—since the fall—we have sought happiness apart from God.[6] We have substituted "vain glory" for "eternal glory," "little brutish pleasure" for "fullness of joy," and "perishing vanities" for "true riches."[7] This has resulted in disorder, meaning we prefer the creature before God, the body before the soul, earth before heaven, and time before eternity.[8] Because of this, we mistake both the end of and means to blessedness.[9]

---

3. Manton does not believe the psalmist's intention in adopting this literary form is to hide some "mystery" for the reader to discover, but simply to aid with "attention and memory." *Psalm 119*, 6:5.

4. Manton, *Psalm 119*, 6:5. Bridges echoes this sentiment: "This most interesting and instructive psalm, like the Psalter itself, opens with a beatitude for our comfort and encouragement, directing us immediately to that happiness, which all mankind in different ways are seeking and inquiring after." *Psalm 119*, 1.

5. Manton, *Psalm 119*, 6:6. Robert Harris agrees, "The end whereto all men are carried, and whereat they aim, is happiness." *The Way of True Happiness, Delivered in Twenty-Four Sermons upon the Beatitudes* (1653; repr., Morgan, Pa.: Soli Deo Gloria, 1998), 10. Similarly, Thomas Watson declares, "Blessedness is the desire of all men." *The Beatitudes: An Exposition of Matthew 5:1–12* (1660; repr., Edinburgh: Banner of Truth, 1994), 24.

6. Thomas Manton, *Sermon on Ecclesiastes 7:29*, in Manton, *Works*, 19:49.

7. Manton, *Sermon on Ecclesiastes 7:29*, 19:51.

8. Manton, *Sermon on Ecclesiastes 7:29*, 19:57–58.

9. Manton, *Psalm 119*, 6:6. According to Watson, "Millions of men mistake both the nature of blessedness and the way thither." *Beatitudes*, 25. Why? They equate

In the century before Manton, John Calvin argued that "all men naturally aspire after happiness, but instead of searching for it in the right path, they designedly prefer wandering up and down through endless by-paths, to their ruin and destruction."[10] He asserted that while everyone seeks "true peace of mind," most err in their pursuit.[11] By way of amplification, Calvin pointed to the Stoics, who believed that blessedness is found in indifference—the impassionate acceptance of circumstances. According to this view, we must learn to desire what is; when we do, we rise above the perturbations of life to experience "peace of mind." Calvin also pointed to the Epicureans, who believed that blessedness is found in indulgence—the incessant gratification of desires. For Epicurus, there are two kinds of pleasure stemming from two kinds of desire: the natural and the vain. We must learn to satisfy our natural desires while denying our vain desires.

These two (Stoicism and Epicureanism) epitomize man's effort to find "true peace of mind," but both proceed on the faulty premise that peace of mind is related to circumstances. For Manton, blessedness flows not from changing circumstances but from an unchanging God.[12] The reason why is obvious: the human soul and "outward things" are mismatched. He explains, "We desire an infinite eternal

---

blessedness with externals. Watson appeals to the example of Solomon to show the folly of believing that happiness is found in "terrestrial things." *Beatitudes*, 25–26. (1) Solomon had parentage; he was the son of David. (2) Solomon had wealth; he "made silver to be in Jerusalem as stones" (1 Kings 10:27). (3) Solomon had luxury; he was surrounded by extravagance—gold, silver, ivory, apes, peacocks, horses, spices, vineyards, music, food, etc. (4) Solomon had power; he "reigned over all the kingdoms from the river unto the land of the Philistines, and unto the border of Egypt: they brought presents, and served Solomon all the days of his life" (1 Kings 4:21). (5) Solomon had pleasure; "he had seven hundred wives, princesses, and three hundred concubines" (1 Kings 11:3). (6) Solomon had wisdom; "And all the earth sought to Solomon, to hear his wisdom, which God had put in his heart" (1 Kings 10:24). In the face of it all, what does Solomon declare? "All was vanity and vexation of spirit" (Eccl. 2:1–11).

10. John Calvin, *Commentary on the Book of Psalms*, trans. James Anderson (Grand Rapids: Baker Books, 2003), 4:403.

11. John Calvin, *Sermons on the Beatitudes*, trans. Robert White (1562; repr., Edinburgh: Banner of Truth, 2006), 18.

12. Manton writes, "True happiness is only to be found in the favor of God, and in the way appointed by God; but man would be at his own dispose, and would invent and

good, still such as may quiet and satisfy us; therefore man being made capable of enjoying God, who is infinite, and finding himself not satisfied with a few or many things, always seeketh after new things. Here is his error, that he seeketh after that which is infinite, among those things which are finite, and so wandereth up and down groping for an eternal good."[13] For Manton, the soul is eternal; it cannot be satisfied by something that is not equal to its own duration—the temporal. In addition, the soul is spiritual; it cannot be satisfied by something that is not equal to its own nature—the material. Finally, the soul is exceptional; it cannot be satisfied by something that is not equal to its own quality—the trivial. The soul can find happiness only in that which is suited to it. This means that the soul can find happiness only in God.

This pursuit of blessedness in God is a central Puritan motif.[14] According to Thomas Watson, "Blessedness lies in the fruition of the chief good. It is not every good that makes man blessed, but it must be the supreme good, and that is God."[15] Robert Harris remarks, "God enjoyed is man's happiness."[16] William Gurnall declares, "Man's happiness stands in his likeness to God, and his fruition of God."[17] Thomas Shepard comments, "There is no man's heart but it must have some good to content it; which good is to be found only in the fountain

---

find out a happiness for himself, and be sufficient to himself for his own blessedness, without any dependence upon God." *Sermon on Ecclesiastes 7:29*, 19:54.

13. Manton, *Sermon on Ecclesiastes 7:29*, 19:56–57.

14. To a man, the Puritans believed that God designed us for a specific *end*—namely, to find pleasure in Him. They found the framework for their view in Aristotle, who asserted, "There is some end (*telos*) of the things we do, which we desire for its own sake." This end is "the chief good" (happiness), which is "always desirable in itself and never for the sake of something else." Aristotle, *Nicomachean Ethics*, in *The Works of Aristotle*, vol. 9, ed. W. D. Ross (Oxford: Oxford University Press, 1963), 1.2, 4, 7. For Aristotle, the conclusion was primarily ethical; that is, the happy person is the virtuous person—virtue being the mean between two extremes. The Puritans, however, while embracing Aristotle's teleological framework, rejected his view of the virtuous man. They made it abundantly clear that our chief good is God.

15. Watson, *Beatitudes*, 29.

16. Harris, *Way of True Happiness*, 18.

17. William Gurnall, *The Christian in Complete Armor: A Treatise of the Saints' War against the Devil* (1662–1665; repr., Edinburgh: Banner of Truth, 1995), 1:415.

of all good, and that is God."[18] For Richard Baxter, "Every soul that hath a title to this rest, doth place his chief happiness in God. This rest consisteth in the full and glorious enjoyment of God."[19] Finally, John Flavel affirms, "God is that supreme good, in the enjoyment of whom all true happiness lies."[20] This Puritan consensus is summed up in the first question of the Westminster Shorter Catechism: "What is the chief end of man?" to which it answers, "Man's chief end is to glorify God, and to enjoy him forever."[21]

Manton stands firmly in this tradition and makes it clear that God is "our chiefest good and our utmost end."[22] That being the case, we must learn how to enjoy Him. For Manton, the way lies in adherence to the following six propositions:

1. God is over all, and above all, blessed enough in himself, and needs nothing from us to add to his happiness and perfection.

2. Though God stand in no need of us, yet he is willing to communicate his blessedness, and to make us happy in the enjoyment of himself.

3. The word of God, especially the gospel part, does only teach us the way how we may be blessed in the enjoyment of God.

4. If we would profit by the word of God, we must go to God, and desire the light and strength of his grace.

---

18. Thomas Shepard, *The Sincere Convert: Discovering the Small Number of True Believers and the Great Difficulty of Saving Conversion*, in *The Sincere Convert and the Sound Believer* (1853; repr., Morgan, Pa.: Soli Deo Gloria, 1999), 62.

19. Richard Baxter, *The Practical Works of Richard Baxter: Select Treatises* (1863; repr., Grand Rapids: Baker, 1981), 54.

20. John Flavel, *The Works of John Flavel* (1820; repr., London: Banner of Truth, 1968), 5:210.

21. According to B. B. Warfield, "The ultimate source of the declaration is almost as easily identified as its proximate source. This must undoubtedly be found in John Calvin, who, in his 'Institutes' and in 'Catechisms' alike, placed this identical idea in the forefront of his instruction." *The Westminster Assembly and Its Work*, in *The Works of Benjamin Warfield* (Grand Rapids: Baker Books, 2003), 6:380.

22. Manton, *Psalm 119*, 6:108.

5. The more we are brought to attend upon the word, and the more influence the word has upon us, the nearer the blessing.

6. It is not only an affront put upon God, but also a great wrong, to neglect the word of God, and the way he prescribes, and to seek blessedness in temporal things.[23]

In the following six chapters, we will unpack each of these propositions in greater detail and consider how they lay the foundation for Manton's spirituality of the Word.

---

23. Manton, *Psalm 119*, 6:111–13.

Chapter 3

The Source of Blessedness

"God is over all, and above all, blessed enough in himself, and needs nothing from us to add to his happiness and perfection."[1] This is Manton's first proposition concerning the way to blessedness. He is adamant that a proper understanding of God is the necessary place to begin. Zophar declares, "Canst thou by searching find out God? canst thou find out the Almighty unto perfection? It is as high as heaven; what canst thou do? deeper than hell; what canst thou know? The measure thereof is longer than the earth, and broader than the sea" (Job 11:7–9). We have a greater chance of holding the stars in the palm of our hand, measuring the mountains on a scale, gathering the oceans in a thimble, and balancing the world's skyscrapers on a needle than we do of finding out "the Almighty unto perfection." God is boundless, whereas our minds are bounded; God is limitless, whereas our minds are limited; God is infinite, whereas our minds are small, sinful, and skewed. Manton's awareness of this leads him to declare, "Finite understandings cannot comprehend him that is infinite, no more than you can empty the sea with a cockleshell. He is the great and only being, in comparison of whom all else is nothing."[2] Despite our inability to

---

1. Manton, *Psalm 119*, 6:111.

2. Manton, *Psalm 119*, 7:84. Manton is not suggesting that God is completely unknowable. In the last century, Karl Barth (1886–1968) introduced the notion of God as "wholly other" to guard against the onslaught of rationalism. Some theologians have taken Barth's statement to an extreme, affirming that God is completely unknowable. Against this trend, we ought to affirm that we can know what God has chosen to reveal concerning Himself in Scripture. He communicates to us through language. If language

know God in His fullness, we can know what He has chosen to reveal concerning Himself.[3]

A Perfect God

For Manton, the starting point for God's self-revelation is the fact that, as the Creator of the universe, He is "over all, and above all."[4] When a builder builds a house, he leaves most of the work in others' hands; but God maintains what He builds. The hand that made everything maintains everything. The power that produced all things out of nothing preserves all things from returning to nothing. God upholds "all things by the word of his power" (Heb. 1:3). How? First, He upholds all things as the foundation on which they stand. He "hangeth the earth upon nothing" (Job 26:7). This means His power is the only pillar that supports it. Second, He upholds all things as the fountain from which they derive their motion. The motions of all His creatures depend on His concurrence. If He were to suspend His influence, the fire would not burn, the eye would not see, the sun would not shine, the wind would not blow, the hand would not move, the bird would not fly, and so on. Third, He upholds all things as the bond by which they hold together. The cosmos does not burst apart, because God is

---

cannot communicate reality, then we cannot know anything about God. For that matter, we cannot know anything about anything.

3. Manton's insistence on God's incomprehensibility should not be confused with the *apophatic* tradition, according to which we must seek communion with God beyond words and thoughts. This communion is known as *hesychasm*—spiritual silence. It stands on the premise that we cannot know anything positively about God; therefore, our access to Him is not rational. The only safe path is the *via negative*—the way of rejection. This "way" involves brief but transforming experiences of union with God. It is developed by following the *Scala Perfectionis*, the stages of perfection: the *purgative* life, which includes renunciation; the *illuminative* life, which includes "learned ignorance" and "the dark night of the soul"; and the *unitive* life, which includes a self-forgetting union with God.

4. Manton cites Rom. 9:5. It is possible that he is also thinking of Eph. 4:6, in which Paul speaks of the "one God and Father of all, who is above all, and through all, and in you all." In short, all things are from Him "in a way of creation," all things are through Him "by way of providential influence and support," and all things are in Him "in their final tendency and result"—namely, His glory. See Manton, *Works*, 1:72; 13:126, 404–5; 20:289.

the principle of cohesion that holds it together. It is impossible for any part of creation to exist for a moment apart from His upholding power. His will makes a thing to be, and His will makes a thing continue to be. He preserves all things from running into confusion or reverting back into nothing.

Manton makes it clear that God did not assume this role (i.e., a new state of being) at the time of creation; rather, God is the eternal Creator. His act of creation is eternal by virtue of the fact that time begins with creation; that is to say, the creation of the universe is not a moment that follows another moment. For Manton, this is of utmost importance when it comes to our understanding of God. Simply put, God is beyond the created universe, including time and space. He knows no past or present but remains in "the same indivisible point of eternity."[5]

Because God has no past or future, He does not experience successive states of being; rather, He "encloseth all being within himself."[6] God does not change, because change requires a cause that makes something to be; there is no cause prior to God. He alone is uncaused. He is "the Father of lights, with whom is no variableness, neither shadow of turning" (James 1:17). The "lights" cast shadows as they move in their orbit, but God is not like that. "The heavenly lights have their vicissitudes, eclipses, and decreases; but our sun shineth always with a like brightness and glory," says Manton.[7] There are no processes active within God's nature that can cause Him to change; moreover, there are no forces outside of God's nature that can cause Him to change.[8] He is "without any motion or change, any local accesses or recesses."[9] As He declared to the people of Malachi's day: "I am the LORD, I change not" (Mal. 3:6). What He was, He is; what He is, He will be.

---

5. Manton, *Psalm 119*, 4:114. See Ex. 3:14–15.
6. Manton, *Psalm 119*, 2:312. See also 7:84.
7. Manton, *Exposition of James*, 4:110.
8. Thomas Manton, *Sermons on Romans 8*, in Manton, *Works*, 12:312.
9. Manton, *Exposition of James*, 4:109.

For Manton, God's immutability is "an attribute that, like a silken string through a chain of pearls, runneth through all the rest."[10] It is of such importance because it declares that God is a perfect being. "There is such an absolute perfection in his nature and being," explains Manton, "that nothing is wanting to it or defective in it, and nothing can be added to it to make it better."[11] God is one, simple, indivisible essence; moreover, His essence is one simple act (infinite and immutable) by which He lives, understands, wills, loves, and so on.[12] Because God is incapable of the least division, it is impossible to distinguish anything within His essence. Therefore, His attributes are not parts of His essence but rather essential properties of His total and complete essence. They can no more be separated from Him than He can be separated from Himself. In other words, God is not merely wise; He is wisdom. He is not merely powerful; He is power. He is not merely good; He is goodness. He is not merely holy; He is holiness. He is not merely just; He is justice. While they are distinguished in their objects and effects, God's attributes are all one in Him—He is perfect being (*summum ens*).

---

10. Manton, *Exposition of James*, 4:113. Manton adds, "The more mutable you are, the less you are like God." *Exposition of James*, 4:114.

11. Manton, *Psalm 119*, 7:236. According to George Swinnock, "A being is absolutely perfect when nothing can be added to it, or taken from it, when it is incapable of the least accession or diminution." *The Works of George Swinnock* (1868; repr., London: Banner of Truth, 1992), 4:391. Swinnock affirms that God is "from himself," His own first cause; "for himself," His own last end; and "by himself," completely independent. *Works*, 4:388–89. He adds, "God is a most pure, simple, unmixed, indivisible essence; he is incapable of the least composition, and therefore of the least division. He is one most pure, one without all parts, members, accidents, and qualities." *Works*, 4:397. For more on the Puritan understanding of God's perfect being, see J. Stephen Yuille, "The Boundless and Blessed God: The Legacy of Amandus Polanus in the Theology of George Swinnock," in *Learning from the Past: Essays on Reception, Catholicity and Dialogue in Honor of Anthony N. S. Lane*, ed. Jon Balserak and Richard Snoddy (London: T&T Clark, 2015), 147–62.

12. For a contemporary study of divine simplicity, see James E. Dolezal, *All That Is in God: Evangelical Theology and the Challenge of Classical Christian Theism* (Grand Rapids: Reformation Heritage Books, 2017).

A Blessed God

Because God is a perfect being, possessing "the fullness of perfection and contentment," He is happy in Himself.[13] According to Manton, "God's blessedness is the fruition of himself, and his delighting in himself."[14] The divine persons delight in each other. The Father has "infinite complacency" in the Son and the Spirit, and the Son in the Father and the Spirit, and the Spirit in the Father and the Son—"all in each, and each in all."[15]

Because God is one, He cannot be divided in "nature and being."[16] Yet there are three who possess "the whole godhead in himself." There are "three ways of existence" in the nature of God because of three "real relations"—namely, "paternity, filiation, and procession."[17] There is, therefore, a distinction between the nature and the three existences. Manton explains that they are "distinct subsistences, distinguished from one another by their unchangeable order of first, second, and third—Father, Word, and Spirit—and their incommunicable properties of paternity, filiation, and procession, or unbegotten, begotten, and proceeding."[18] God revealed this when the Father sent the Son and the Spirit into the world; that is, God made Himself known in the "missions" of the Son and the Spirit, which reveal that God's life takes place in eternal relations of origin. The Father sends the Son and the Spirit in time because the Son and the Spirit proceed from the Father in eternity (John 8:42; 15:26). The Father sends the Son because the Son stands in an eternal relation of origin with regard to the Father (i.e., generation), and the Father sends the Spirit because the Spirit stands in an eternal relation of origin with regard to the Father (i.e., spiration).

Because God is a perfect being whose life takes place in relations of origin in "the same indivisible point of eternity," He is necessarily sufficient and satisfied in Himself; thus, His "happiness lies in knowing

---

13. Manton, *Psalm 119*, 6:108. See Rom. 9:5; 1 Tim. 1:11; 6:15.
14. Manton, *Psalm 119*, 6:109.
15. Manton, *Psalm 119*, 6:111.
16. Thomas Manton, *Sermons on John 17*, in Manton, *Works*, 10:158.
17. Manton, *Sermons on John 17*, 10:158.
18. Manton, *Sermons on John 17*, 10:160.

himself, in loving himself, in delighting in himself."[19] Do we have any effect on this blessed God? "He is above our benefits and injuries," says Manton.[20] Because God is "above all, and over all," He does not require anything outside of Himself, nor does He benefit from anything outside of Himself. He is His own blessedness.

For Manton, this is the essential starting point on the way to blessedness. In a word, we must acknowledge with the psalmist, "Blessed art thou, O LORD" (Ps. 119:12).[21]

---

19. Manton, *Psalm 119*, 6:109.

20. Manton, *Psalm 119*, 6:111.

21. Manton explains that God is blessed "objectively" because He is the object of our blessedness and "subjectively" in an active sense (because He is blessed in Himself) or passive sense (because He is blessed by us). *Psalm 119*, 6:108–10.

Chapter 4

The End of Blessedness

Manton has established in his first "proposition" that God is "blessed enough in himself, and needs nothing from us." This "blessed" God does "marvellous things without number" (Job 5:9). What are we to Him? Do we have any effect on Him? Does He need us or gain anything from us? "Can a man be profitable unto God?" (Job 22:2). For Manton, the answer is a resounding no, but he does not leave it at that: "Though God stand in no need of us, yet he is willing to communicate his blessedness, and to make us happy in the enjoyment of himself."[1] This is Manton's second proposition concerning the way to the enjoyment of God's blessedness.

God's Goodness

Since God is a perfect being, He is sufficient and satisfied in Himself, thereby making Him the chief good. God is originally, supremely, infinitely, and eternally good.[2] At times, the Bible compares God to that good which is *essential* to us: He is life, light, food, water, and rest.[3] At times, it compares God to that good which is *beneficial* to us: He is home, health, peace, fire, and refuge.[4] And at times it compares God to that good which is *delightful* to us: He is wealth, honor, wine, joy,

---

1. Manton, *Psalm 119*, 6:111. Bridges echoes this sentiment: "[God] is 'blessed' in himself, and delights to communicate his blessedness to his people." *Psalm 119*, 25.

2. Manton, *Psalm 119*, 7:107–9.

3. See Pss. 36:9; 116:7; John 1:4, 9; 4:10; 6:51; James 1:17.

4. See Pss. 42:11; 57:1; 90:9–10; Zech. 2:5; 2 Cor. 13:11.

and pleasure.[5] "Thou art good, and doest good," declares the psalmist (Ps. 119:68).[6] In his sermon on this verse, Manton maintains that we must think of God's goodness in three ways.

First, God is "naturally" good.[7] "There is," says Manton, "such an absolute perfection in his nature and being, that nothing is wanting to it or defective in it, and nothing can be added to it to make it better." He is "originally" good—good of Himself. He is "essentially" good—good in Himself. He is "infinitely" good—"the gathering together of goodness." And He is "immutably" good—"there can be no addition made to him, so no subtraction."[8] In a word, God is "good of himself, good in himself, yea, good itself."[9]

Second, God is "morally" good.[10] His goodness is seen in all His perfections. He is good in what He says (truthfulness); He is good in what He does (faithfulness); He is good in His condemnation of sinners (righteousness); He is good in His justification of sinners (lovingkindness). He is "the fountain and pattern of all that virtuous goodness which is in the creatures."[11]

Third, God is "beneficially" good.[12] He diffuses His goodness "as the sun doth light, or as the fountain poureth out waters."[13] How? For starters, God communicates His goodness to us "mediately" in the present through secondary means. These include common mercies such as life, light, warmth, and health, which He gives through the sun, rain, plants, and animals. "God poureth out his influences to the

---

5. See Job 22:24–25; Ps. 43:4; Isa. 25:6; 33:21; Zech. 2:5.

6. For Stephen Charnock, "The goodness of God…renders him beautiful, and his beauty renders him lovely…. This is the most powerful attractive, and masters the affections of the soul." *Discourses upon the Existence and Attributes of God* (1853; repr., Grand Rapids: Baker, 1990), 2:330.

7. Manton, *Psalm 119*, 7:236. See Mark 10:18. See also *Sermons on Romans 8*, 12:276.

8. Manton, *Psalm 119*, 7:236. For the same fourfold division, see 7:243.

9. Manton, *Psalm 119*, 7:236. See also 7:107–9.

10. Manton, *Psalm 119*, 7:236. See Ex. 33:19; Ps. 25:8. See also *Sermons on Romans 8*, 12:277.

11. Manton, *Psalm 119*, 7:236.

12. Manton, *Psalm 119*, 7:236. See Gen. 17:1; Ps. 84:11. See also *Sermons on Romans 8*, 12:277.

13. Manton, *Psalm 119*, 7:237.

heavens, and the heavens pour out their influences upon the earth," says Manton.[14] These secondary means also include special mercies such as grace, comfort, peace, and joy, which God gives through the Word and sacraments.[15] In addition, God communicates His goodness to us "immediately" in the future without the use of secondary means.[16] This is the happiness of heaven, where we will enjoy "immediate influences from God."[17] Our knowledge of Him will be full and perfect, constant and complete, resulting in hitherto unknown delight as we rest fully and finally in Him. In a word, God will be "all in all" (1 Cor. 15:28).[18]

---

14. Manton, *Psalm 119*, 6:112.

15. Manton, *Psalm 119*, 6:112. For Manton, God does not communicate His mercies to the soul apart from the Word and sacraments. This stands in marked contrast to the popular notion that God communicates directly to the soul. According to Watchman Nee, for example, the individual is composed of three parts: body (the outermost man), soul (the outer man), and spirit (the inner man). Watchman Nee, *The Release of the Spirit* (Bombay: Gospel Literature Service, 1965), 24. Our thoughts and emotions belong to our soul (the outer man). Therefore, they do not share the same nature with God. Only our spirit (the inner man) relates to God. This means that our soul must be "broken" to release our spirit. We must practice God's presence to such a degree that our spirit and the Spirit become indistinguishable. "The release of the spirit is the release of the human spirit as well as the release of the Holy Spirit, who is in the spirit of man. Since the Holy Spirit and our spirit are joined into one, they can be distinguished only in name, not in fact." Nee, *Release of the Spirit*, 21. This form of mysticism is common within evangelicalism; however, it is usually found in a far more subtle form—the belief that there is a "fusion" (ontologically speaking) between our spirit and the Spirit whereby we attain an immediate knowledge of God. That is to say, we sense the Holy Spirit working directly (apart from the Bible) on our spirit, producing impulses and intuitions as a means of conveying His will to us.

16. Manton, *Psalm 119*, 6:112. Manton states, "In blessedness there is a confluence of all good; our joys are full and eternal. There is the immediate sight and presence of God, and Jesus Christ, who shall be all in all to them.... We are brought into the presence of him who is blessedness itself." *The Transfiguration of Christ*, in Manton, *Works*, 1:375. See John 17:24; 1 Cor. 13:12.

17. Manton, *Psalm 119*, 6:112. See also 7:237. For more on our happiness upon seeing God, see Thomas Manton, *Sermons on 2 Corinthians 5*, in Manton, *Works*, 13:23–25; and *Sermons on Titus 2:11–14*, in Manton, *Works*, 16:194–98.

18. Manton explains that we do not become "partakers of the divine nature" in terms of God's essence but "his communicable excellencies." We will be like Him in

The Communication of God's Goodness

Manton believed that the present communication of God's spiritual mercies involves a spiritual correspondence between God and us whereby He lets forth influences on our souls and we respond to Him.[19] How does this happen?[20]

First, God demonstrates that He is "good, and doeth good" in creation.[21] His power is evident in the fact that He created the heavens and the earth out of nothing; His wisdom in His ordination and governance of all things; and His goodness in His filling the earth with plants and animals, the sea with fish, and the heavens with stars.[22] For Manton, "The creation is nothing else but an effusion of the bounty and goodness of God. He made the world, not that he might be happy, but that he might be liberal." God was blessed without us, enjoying an

---

holiness and happiness, for He is "a holy and happy being." *Sermon on 2 Peter 1:4*, in Manton, *Works*, 2:214, 218.

19. John Owen explains, "Our communion, then, with God consisteth in his communication of himself unto us, with our returnal unto him of that which he requireth and accepteth, flowing from that union which in Jesus Christ we have with him." *The Works of John Owen*, ed. William H. Goold (1850–1853; repr., Edinburgh: Banner of Truth, 1974), 2:8–9. In his treatise *Of Communion with God*, Owen considers the Christian's communion with the Father in love, with the Son in grace, and with the Spirit in consolation. He comments, "The way and means, then, on the part of the saints, whereby in Christ they enjoy communion with God, are all the spiritual and holy actings and outgoings of their souls in those graces, and by those ways, wherein both the moral and instituted worship of God doth consist. Faith, love, trust, joy, etc., are the natural or moral worship of God, whereby those in whom they are have communion with him." *Works of John Owen*, 2:11.

20. John Flavel is helpful in his treatment of this subject. He identifies a threefold path to communion with God. (1) There is communion with God "in the contemplation of the Divine attributes, and the impressions God makes by them upon our souls, whilst we meditate on them." (2) There is communion with God "in the exercises of our graces in the various duties of religion; in praying, hearing, sacraments, &c. in all which the Spirit of the Lord influences the graces of his people, and they return the fruits thereof in some measure to him. As God hath planted various graces in regenerate souls, so he hath appointed various duties to exercise and draw forth those graces; and when they do so, then have his people sweet actual communion with him." (3) There is communion with God "in the way of his providences." *Works of John Flavel*, 4:240–45.

21. Manton, *Psalm 119*, 7:238. See Gen. 1:31. See also *Sermons on Romans 8*, 12:277.

22. Manton, *Psalm 119*, 7:85.

absolute sufficiency within Himself; therefore, He did not create for His own benefit, but for our benefit. His great aim was "to raise up objects out of nothing, to whom he would communicate his goodness."[23]

Second, God demonstrates that He is "good, and doeth good" in providence.[24] His power is evident in the management of providence, His wisdom in the order of providence, and His goodness in the effects of providence.[25] God's providential goodness is twofold. First, it is general to His creatures: "The LORD is good to all: and his tender mercies are over all his works" (Ps. 145:9).[26] He bestows common blessings such as life, health, wealth, and strength on all. Second, it is peculiar to His children: "The LORD is good unto them that wait for him, to the soul that seeketh him" (Lam. 3:25). God leads them "to their everlasting hopes, and that estate which they expect in the world to come, where, in the arms of God, they shall be blessed for evermore."[27]

Third, God demonstrates that He is "good, and doeth good" in redemption.[28] In the gospel, we see God's wisdom in His orderly disposal of the covenant of grace, and we see His power in Christ's incarnation and resurrection. But, far eclipsing these, we see God's love and goodness.[29] He communicates these to us by providing "a remedy for lost sinners."[30] "Great are thy tender mercies, O LORD" (Ps. 119:156).[31] According to Manton, God's mercy is "infinite, as his nature is; but in the effects as to us there is a great difference."[32] God's "general mercy"

---

23. Manton, *Psalm 119*, 7:85. See Rev. 4:11.

24. Manton, *Psalm 119*, 7:238. See also *Sermons on Romans 8*, 12:278.

25. Manton, *Psalm 119*, 7:87.

26. See also Matt. 5:45; Acts 14:17.

27. Manton, *Psalm 119*, 7:239.

28. Manton, *Psalm 119*, 7:238. See Rom. 5:8; Titus 3:4; 1 John 4:9–10. See also Manton, *Sermons on Romans 8*, 12:278.

29. Manton, *Psalm 119*, 7:86. For more on Manton's thoughts on God's love, see *Sermon on John 3:16*, in Manton, *Works*, 2:340–57.

30. Manton, *Psalm 119*, 7:238.

31. See Ps. 62:12; Isa. 28:21; Mic. 7:18; 2 Cor. 1:3.

32. Manton, *Psalm 119*, 9:160. See also Manton, *Exposition of Jude*, in Manton, *Works*, 5:57–67.

is toward all creatures, whereby He sustains them.[33] God's "special mercy" is toward all people, whereby He assists them in their misery.[34] But God's "peculiar mercy" is toward His elect in Christ, which is the greatest mercy of all,[35] for by it God pardons our sins and receives us into a state of favor.[36] "We were unworthy and miserable sinners," declares Manton, "[but] then his eye pitied us and his hand saved us." We commit innumerable sins and bear innumerable miseries, but God's mercies are far greater.[37] His mercy is so great that He sent His Son to die for us.[38] "If all the compassions of all fathers and mothers were joined together," says Manton, "it were nothing to God; he is the father of mercies (James 5:11)."[39]

God impresses these three expressions of His goodness (creation, providence, and redemption) on us, thereby communicating His blessedness to us.[40] As a result, a "deep sense" of His goodness overwhelms

---

33. Manton, *Psalm 119*, 9:161. See Ps. 145:5. For more on Manton's understanding of God's general love and special (peculiar) love, see *Sermons on Romans 8*, 12:345–46.

34. Manton, *Psalm 119*, 9:160. See Titus 3:4. Elsewhere, Manton writes, "There is a twofold love in God—the love of benevolence and complacency. The elect from all eternity are loved by God with a love of benevolence, whereby he willed good unto them, and decrees to bestow good upon them; but the love of complacency and delight is that love whereby God accepteth us, delighteth in us, when he hath made us lovely as his own children, reconciled them by the death of Christ, renewed them by the Spirit of Christ, and furnished them with all the graces which make us acceptable to him, and precious in his sight." *Transfiguration of Christ*, 1:385.

35. Manton, *Psalm 119*, 9:160. See Rom. 9:15.

36. Manton, *Psalm 119*, 9:161. See 1 Tim. 1:13; 1 Peter 1:3.

37. Manton, *Psalm 119*, 9:164.

38. Manton, *Psalm 119*, 9:164. See 1 John 4:9–10.

39. Manton, *Psalm 119*, 9:162.

40. Swinnock places tremendous emphasis on the pursuit of knowledge. Without it, the soul is a "dungeon of darkness and blackness"—full of confusion. *Works of George Swinnock*, 4:481. Elsewhere, he writes, "They who know the infiniteness and immensity of [God's] being, cannot but…esteem all things as nothing to Him," "they who know the power of God cannot but fear Him, and stand in awe of His presence," "they who know the eternity of God, will choose Him before temporal vanities," "they who know the wisdom of God will submit to His providences, and acquiesce in all His dispensations," "they who know the faithfulness of God will credit His word, and make Him the object of their hope and faith," "they who know the mercy, and love, and goodness of God, will love, and admire, and trust, and praise Him," "they who know the holiness

us. Manton describes it as "the complacency and well-pleasedness of the soul in God as an all-sufficient portion."[41] This causes us to respond to Him. For starters, we respond in humility.[42] A sight of His goodness "abaseth and lesseneth" all things in "affection and estimation."[43] Second, we respond in faith.[44] When we feel the guilt of our sin and the weight of His wrath, we turn to a good God. His goodness is the fountain of our "hope, strength, and consolation."[45] Third, we respond in repentance.[46] We see our sin as an abusing and despising of infinite goodness. Fourth, we respond in love.[47] We "love him because of the goodness and amiableness of his nature, because of his bounty in our creation, redemption, and daily providence, and because he will be our God forever."[48]

Conclusion

For Manton, this is what it means to take God as our "portion" (Ps. 119:57).[49] As he explains, the term *portion* comes from the distribution of the land of Canaan to the Israelites, and it serves to convey the reality that God alone is our inheritance. Being spiritual, our soul "must have a spiritual good." Being immortal, our soul "must have an immortal

---

of God will sanctify Him in their approaches to Him, and walk humbly and watchfully with Him," and "they who know the anger of God will stand in awe, and not sin." *Works of George Swinnock*, 3:154–55. Swinnock exhorts, "Reader, be persuaded, therefore, to study this knowledge of God; think no labor too much for it; pray, and read, and hear, and confer, and mourn that thou mayest know God." *Works of George Swinnock*, 3:158.

41. Manton, *Sermons on Romans 8*, 12:278.
42. For Manton on humility, see *Sermon on Micah 6:8*, in Manton, *Works*, 15:404–13.
43. Manton, *Psalm 119*, 7:241.
44. For Manton's understanding of faith, see *Sermons on 2 Corinthians 5*, 13:346–53.
45. Manton, *Psalm 119*, 7:242.
46. Manton, *Psalm 119*, 7:242.
47. Manton, *Psalm 119*, 7:243.
48. Manton, *Psalm 119*, 7:244.
49. See Pss. 73:26; 142:5. "Delight in the Lord as our portion, naturally leads us to entreat His favor as 'life.'… Any indulged indolence, or neglect, or unfaithfulness— relaxing our diligence, and keeping back the whole heart from God—will, indeed, never fail to remove the sunshine from the soul.… You may, indeed, be a child of God without the enjoyment of the blessing; but not so, if you be content to be without it." Bridges, *Psalm 119*, 144–45.

good."[50] But, above all else, our soul must have a satisfying good. God satisfies all of our needs. He is satisfied in Himself, and there is more than enough in Him to fill us. After all, "that which fills an ocean will fill a bucket."[51]

When we take God as our portion, we find in Him all we could ever want: an eternal and spiritual good, suitable to our every need. This is the sum and substance of all the promises: "[I] will be their God, and they shall be my people" (Jer. 31:33). This promise is heaven—the very heaven of heavens: "In thy presence is fulness of joy; at thy right hand there are pleasures for evermore" (Ps. 16:11). This, for Manton, is the second step on the way to blessedness: the blessed God is willing "to communicate his blessedness, and to make us happy in the enjoyment of himself." He is "our God for ever and ever" (Ps. 48:14). He is not our God for a day, week, month, or year, but "for ever and ever." He is not our God for a thousand years, but "for ever and ever." He is not our God for a million years, but "for ever and ever." In sum, "Happy is that people...whose God is the LORD" (Ps. 144:15).

---

50. Manton, *Psalm 119*, 7:110–11.

51. Manton, *Psalm 119*, 7:112. Manton adds, "The soul is like a sponge, always thirsting, and seeking of something from without to be filled—a chaos of desires. Man was made to live in dependence." *Psalm 119*, 7:116.

Chapter 5

The Means of Blessedness

God makes us happy in the enjoyment of Him by impressing His goodness on us, our knowledge of which comes by way of creation, providence, and (primarily) redemption. But how do we learn of God's goodness in redemption? This question leads Manton to his third proposition: "The word of God, especially the gospel part, does only teach us the way how we may be blessed in the enjoyment of God."[1] For Manton, God is incomprehensible. "O the depth of the riches both of the wisdom and knowledge of God! how unsearchable are his judgments, and his ways past finding out!" (Rom. 11:33). Because God is infinite, His wisdom and knowledge are measureless. He knows what was, what is, what will be, what can be, and what cannot be. By one pure, simple, eternal act of His infinite understanding, He knows all things perfectly, immediately, and distinctly—at every moment. How can we know this God? For Manton, the answer is God's Word. Because it leads us to "the fruition of God," it is incomparably better than anything else. Simply put, it is "the next object to God, fit for our love."[2] For this reason, we proclaim with the psalmist, "O how love I thy law!" (Ps. 119:97).

---

1. Manton, *Psalm 119*, 6:112.

2. Manton, *Psalm 119*, 9:234. "No man has taken the first step towards real, abiding blessedness until he has become a sincere and habitual servant of the Most High God according to Scripture." Plumer, *Psalms*, 1024.

The Author of Scripture

We love the Word because of its author:[3] it is "not the word of a weak man, but of a great and mighty God."[4] Moreover, it is His "epistle and love-letter to our souls."[5] When we perceive this, we echo the psalmist's affirmation: "Thy testimonies are wonderful" (Ps. 119:129). They are wonderful in their "majesty and composure";[6] God's authority is evident in almost every line. They are wonderful in their "matter and depth of mystery."[7] Here we discover truth concerning the glory of God, the creation of the world, the fall of man, and the work of Christ. His testimonies are wonderful in their "purity and perfection";[8] they reveal the perfect will of God, which reaches "to the very soul and all the motions of the heart." They are wonderful in their "harmony and consent of all the parts."[9] All of Scripture serves one great end— namely, "the glorifying of God's grace and mercy in those that are saved, and his justice in those that are damned."[10] God's testimonies are wonderful in their power.[11] Scripture not only fills the head with notions but "pierces the heart," "alarms the conscience," and "awakens the affections."[12] It possesses power to humble and terrify, convert and transform, comfort and confirm.[13]

The Matter of Scripture

We also love God's Word because of its matter.[14] It deals with "everlasting concernments";[15] moreover, it possesses all those properties that delight our hearts, thereby drawing us to it. For starters, it is true.

---

3. Manton, *Psalm 119*, 7:464.
4. Manton, *Psalm 119*, 9:172.
5. Manton, *Psalm 119*, 7:464.
6. Manton, *Psalm 119*, 8:335.
7. Manton, *Psalm 119*, 8:336.
8. Manton, *Psalm 119*, 8:337.
9. Manton, *Psalm 119*, 8:337.
10. Manton, *Psalm 119*, 8:338.
11. Manton, *Psalm 119*, 8:338.
12. Manton, *Psalm 119*, 8:338.
13. Manton, *Psalm 119*, 8:340–42.
14. Manton, *Psalm 119*, 7:464.
15. Manton, *Psalm 119*, 9:173.

According to Manton, "Truth is the good of the understanding, and without the knowledge of which we can have no tranquility of mind."[16] Scripture is also good: "There is a double desire in man...to know the truth, and to enjoy the chiefest good; the happiness...of the understanding, that lies in the contemplation of truth; and the happiness of the will in the enjoyment of good."[17] Manton refers to these (truth and goodness) as "light and life"—"the two great things man looks after as a reasonable creature." We are never happy until these two desires are satisfied. In Manton's estimation, they are satisfied in God's Word because it is there that we discover the "*primum verum*, the supreme truth, and *summum bonum*, the chief good."[18]

We love God's Word not only because it is true and good but because it is profound. "There is," says Manton, "a curiosity of knowledge" whereby we seek "what is rare and profound."[19] This profundity is found in Scripture alone. Peter informs us that the gospel contains "things the angels desire to look into" (1 Peter 1:12); they long to understand the fullness of salvation. We find this phrase in Luke 24:12, where we read that Peter was "stooping down" to see into the empty tomb. He had to bend down to get the view he wanted. That is what the angels are doing as they investigate salvation.[20] They live with "the blessed vision and constant fruition of God," yet they are taken up in the study of the gospel. They enjoy "a happy state," but they are "finite, capable of being improved, and that by the doctrine of the holy Scriptures."[21] If that is true of the angels, what does it mean for us? In brief, it means that God's Word is an inexhaustible mine of treasure.

The Use of Scripture

Finally, we love God's Word because of its use. It increases our knowledge of Him and converts the soul.[22] God uses it to bring us back

---

16. Manton, *Psalm 119*, 7:464. See Ps. 19:9; John 17:17; Eph. 1:13.
17. Manton, *Psalm 119*, 7:466.
18. Manton, *Psalm 119*, 7:466.
19. Manton, *Psalm 119*, 7:468.
20. Manton, *Exposition of James*, 4:161.
21. Manton, *Psalm 119*, 7:469.
22. Manton, *Psalm 119*, 7:469. See Ps. 19:7, 10.

to Himself; more specifically, He uses it to break our hearts for sin and then to heal us.[23] For Manton, this healing process rests on two key truths.

The first is reconciliation with God.[24] How can those who are "obnoxious to the wrath of God" enjoy "delightful communion with him"? For Manton, this is the fundamental question. Until it is resolved, our hearts are never settled. Scripture resolves it as follows: "God was in Christ, reconciling the world unto himself, not imputing their trespasses unto them" (2 Cor. 5:19).[25] Manton believes "there is more glory in these few words, and more of God discovered in them, than there is in all the world.... That short sentence discovers more of God's intentions and good-will to man than all the bounty of his providence in and by all the creatures put together."[26] It declares that God reconciles sinners to Himself through Christ.[27] But how? For Manton, the answer resides in Isaiah 53:5: "But he was wounded for our transgressions, he was bruised for our iniquities: the chastisement of our peace was upon him; and with his stripes we are healed." Here Manton points to Christ's penal substitutionary sacrifice as the only means of reconciliation with God. Scripture declares this hope, thereby healing the brokenhearted.

The second truth is eternal salvation.[28] God's Word teaches that Christ has "abolished death" and "brought life and immortality to light

---

23. Manton, *Psalm 119*, 7:264.

24. Manton, *Psalm 119*, 7:467.

25. For Manton's full treatment of this verse, see *Sermons on 2 Corinthians 5*, 13:271–89.

26. Manton, *Psalm 119*, 7:467.

27. Manton treats of this subject in two sermons on Ps. 32:1–2. He remarks, "Now, happy we cannot be but in God, who is the only, immutable, eternal, and all-sufficient good, which satisfies and fills up all the capacities and desires of our souls. And we are debarred from access to him by sin, which hath made a breach and separation between him and us, and till that be taken away there can be no converse, and sin can only be taken away by God's pardon." *Sermon 1 on Psalm 32:1–2*, in Manton, *Works*, 2:177. According to Manton, David speaks of "filth to be covered, a burden of which we must be eased, and a debt that must be cancelled." He adds, "Unless this be, what a miserable condition are we in!" (2:184). We enter "the evangelical state" through faith and repentance (2:192).

28. Manton, *Psalm 119*, 7:468.

through the gospel" (2 Tim. 1:10). Thus, it alone can make us "wise unto salvation" (2 Tim. 3:15). Manton remarks,

> Wisdom lies in fixing a right end, in a choice of fit means, and in a dexterous prosecution of those means for the attainment of this end. Now the holy Scriptures make you wise to salvation—that is, to fix upon a right end, for they discover that there is a happiness that we may fix upon, and they direct us in the way; and then by mighty and potent methods of reasoning they quicken and awaken us to look after this business, that we may dexterously pursue it as the great care that lies upon us; therefore the children of God delight in the word, because this makes them wise to salvation.[29]

This wisdom (i.e., reconciliation with God and eternal life) brings us into a blessed condition.[30] For Manton, it means that we are blessed in six ways.[31] First, we are "freed from wrath" and possess "the blessedness of a pardoned man";[32] consequently, we are "out of danger of perishing."[33] Second, we are "taken into favor and respect with God." There is a "real friendship" between God and us, "not only in point of harmony and agreement of mind, but mutual delight and fellowship with each other."[34] Third, we are "under the special care and conduct of God's providence." He overrules all our conditions for good. In a word, our "blessings are sanctified" and our "miseries are unstinged."[35] Fourth, we have "a sure covenant-right to everlasting glory." We rejoice in hope of the glory of God because we are heirs of God.[36] Fifth, we have "sweet experiences of God's goodness" in this world. His presence with us,

---

29. Manton, *Psalm 119*, 7:468.

30. For more on Manton's insights regarding God's wisdom in the way of salvation, see his sermon on Matt. 11:18–19, "Wisdom Is Justified in Her Children," in Manton, *Works*, 2:93–112.

31. Manton, *Psalm 119*, 6:14–15.

32. Manton, *Psalm 119*, 6:14. See John 5:24.

33. Manton, *Psalm 119*, 6:14.

34. Manton, *Psalm 119*, 6:14. See John 15:14.

35. Manton, *Psalm 119*, 6:14–15. See Rom. 8:28; 1 Cor. 3:23.

36. Manton, *Psalm 119*, 6:14. See 1 John 3:1.

and our sense of His love for us, eclipses "all worldly joys."[37] Sixth, we have "a great deal of peace." The God of peace is ours; therefore, we are "assured of his love and favorable acceptance." "If he smiles on us," says Manton, "it is enough, though all the world should be against us."[38]

Conclusion

It is God's Word alone ("especially the gospel part") that reveals His goodness; therefore, His Word alone teaches us "the way how we may be blessed in the enjoyment of God."[39] Paul speaks of "the glorious gospel of the blessed God" (1 Tim. 1:11). With this verse in mind, Manton affirms that the law is good, but the gospel is glorious because it displays "more of the glory of God."[40] It reveals that there is a way "how we may come to be blessed in God, how he may with respect to us be a fountain of blessedness."[41] That being the case, we must take God's Word as our "heritage for ever" (Ps. 119:111). We must esteem it above all else to be our happiness. In the words of Manton, it is our "wealth," "treasure," and "chief estate."[42] It is, first of all, a full heritage, in that it is perfect. Nothing can be added to it or subtracted from it. "Here is God made over to us; the great blessing of the covenant is, I am thy God."[43] It is, second, a sure heritage, in that it is certain. Nothing can change it. "God is very tender of his word, more than of heaven and earth."[44] It is, third, a durable heritage, in that it is eternal: "It is better than riches than all the world, for then our right to God and eternal life still remaineth."[45]

---

37. Manton, *Psalm 119*, 6:15. See Ps. 17:15.

38. Manton, *Psalm 119*, 9:207.

39. Manton affirms, "All practical divinity may be reduced to these three heads, a sense of our misery by nature, a flying to God by Christ for a remedy, and the life of love and praise, which becometh Christ's reconciled and redeemed ones. This is repentance." *Sermon on Acts 17:30–31*, in Manton, *Works*, 16:405.

40. Manton, *Psalm 119*, 6:112.

41. Manton, *Psalm 119*, 6:112.

42. Manton, *Psalm 119*, 8:136.

43. Manton, *Psalm 119*, 8:137. See Ps. 16:5; Rom. 8:17; 1 Cor. 3:21.

44. Manton, *Psalm 119*, 8:139.

45. Manton, *Psalm 119*, 8:140.

Because God's Word is our heritage, we live on it. It is the ground of our future hope and the storehouse for our present supply.[46] It shows us how "we might at length be happy in his love."[47] It tells us that "we have an interest in the eternal God, and we shall live eternally to enjoy him. God lives forever, and we live forever, that we may enjoy God."[48]

---

46. Manton, *Psalm 119*, 8:137.
47. Manton, *Psalm 119*, 7:7.
48. Manton, *Psalm 119*, 8:140. See Ps. 73:26.

Chapter 6

The Pursuit of Blessedness

Manton makes it clear that God's Word ("especially the gospel part") reveals the way to the enjoyment of God's blessedness because it reveals the means of reconciliation with Him and thus the means to eternal life. To this he adds his fourth proposition: "If we would profit by the word of God, we must go to God, and desire the light and strength of his grace."[1] Because God's Word is ineffectual apart from God Himself, we must seek His assistance to understand it. Manton elaborates,

> If we would enjoy the blessed God, according to the direction of his word, we must not only consult with the word, but with God. Nothing else can draw us off from the world, and persuade us to look after heavenly things; nothing else will teach us the vanity of the creature, the reality of spiritual privileges. Until we see these things in a divine light, the heart hangs off from God.... We shall still run after lying vanities until God doth open our eyes to see the mysteries of the Word, and to be affected with the way.[2]

We are persuaded of "heavenly things" only as God Himself instructs us. Christ confirms this very thing, declaring, "It is written in the prophets, And they shall be all taught of God. Every man therefore that hath heard, and hath learned of the Father, cometh unto me" (John 6:45). Here, Christ quotes from Jeremiah 31:34: "And they shall

---

1. Manton, *Psalm 119*, 6:113. This proposition is derived from Ps. 16:7 and John 6:44.

2. Manton, *Psalm 119*, 6:113.

teach no more every man his neighbour, and every man his brother, saying, Know the LORD: for they shall all know me, from the least of them unto the greatest of them, saith the LORD."[3] The inference is that God Himself is our Teacher. The way to the enjoyment of His blessedness is found in His Word, but that Word remains a closed book without His instruction. Aware of this, the psalmist prays, "Blessed art thou, O LORD: teach me thy statutes" (Ps. 119:12).[4]

The Need for Divine Teaching

We need God to teach us His Word because we are incapable of arriving at the knowledge of His truth on our own.[5] Why? The first reason is our blindness—the "weakness of a natural understanding."[6] Paul declares, "But the natural man receiveth not the things of the Spirit of God: for they are foolishness unto him: neither can he know them, because they are spiritually discerned" (1 Cor. 2:14). The term *natural* refers to what belongs to fallen human nature. We might be learned, educated, scientific, intellectual, and refined yet unable to discern spiritual truth. Thus, God must teach us: "Divine things cannot be seen but by a divine light, and spiritual things by a spiritual light, else they shall have no savor and relish."[7]

The second reason we need divine instruction is our forgetfulness. We are "apt to forsake" what we know concerning the things of God.[8] By this, Manton does not mean that we forget notionally, no longer remembering what we once knew.[9] He means that we forget "affec-

---

3. See also Isa. 54:13.

4. This emphasis on divine instruction is a central motif in Ps. 119. This is evident in the frequency of the psalmist's twofold request: "Teach me" (vv. 12, 26, 33, 64, 66, 68, 108, 124, 135) and "Give me understanding" (vv. 27, 34, 73, 144, 169).

5. J. I. Packer describes this predicament as follows: "Sin within us leads to an unresponsiveness to spiritual truth and reality that the New Testament calls hardness and blindness of heart…only the illumination of the Holy Spirit, opening our heart to God's Word and God's Word to our hearts, can bring understanding of, conviction about, and consent to, the things that God declares." *Quest for Godliness*, 83.

6. Manton, *Psalm 119*, 6:116. See also 6:52–53; 8:279.

7. Manton, *Psalm 119*, 6:116.

8. Manton, *Psalm 119*, 6:117.

9. Manton, *Psalm 119*, 8:115. See also 6:153–54.

tively," meaning we are no longer "answerably affected" by what we know.[10] In other words, the truth does not impact the way we live.

The third reason we need divine instruction is our stubbornness. In the garden of Eden, Adam's chief good and last end was God. But Adam rebelled, yielding to Satan's temptation: "Ye shall be as gods" (Gen. 3:5). As a result, man fell from his original condition. His fallen human nature is known as the flesh—that which is oriented toward self-love, self-autonomy, self-sufficiency, and self-gratification. "When man fell from God," writes Manton, "he fell to himself."[11] Ever since, the flesh has alienated us from God. It enslaves us, darkening our minds, hardening our hearts, and binding our wills. As a result, "the whole business of Christianity seems to be a foolish thing to a carnal heart."[12] The flesh is at war with God and, therefore, unable to obey God and unable to please God: "God hath made man upright; but they have sought out many inventions" (Eccl. 7:29). We are full of "crooked counsels," "abominable errors," "mistakes," "lusts," and "passions."[13]

The Means of Divine Teaching

Each of these factors means that we are entirely dependent on God to lead us in the way of blessedness.[14] He does this by declaring "his mind" in Scripture, appointing the public ministry of His Word, and imparting His Spirit to us.[15] Manton remarks, "The Scripture is our external light, as the sun is to the world; the understanding is our internal light. Now this eye is become blind in all natural men, and in the best it is most imperfect; therefore the eyes of the understanding must be opened by the spirit of wisdom and revelation (Ephesians 1:17–18). Though truths be plainly revealed by the Spirit of God in Scripture, yet

---

10. Manton, *Psalm 119*, 8:115.
11. Manton, *Sermon on Galatians 5:16*, in Manton, *Works*, 2:287.
12. Manton, *Psalm 119*, 6:117.
13. Manton, *Psalm 119*, 6:341.
14. See Ps. 119:12, 26, 27, 29, 33, 34, 64, 66, 73, 108, 124, 125, 135, 144, 169.
15. Manton, *Psalm 119*, 6:115.

there must be a removal of that natural darkness and blindness that is upon our understandings."[16]

Because we are ignorant (in mind) and impotent (in will), we need "a double assistance from God."[17] By His "efficacious teaching" He cures "the blindness of our minds" and inclines "our hearts towards spiritual and heavenly things."[18]

Illumination

God illumines the mind so that we apprehend things in a "spiritual manner."[19] The psalmist prays, "Open thou mine eyes, that I may behold wondrous things out of thy law" (Ps. 119:18). For Manton, there is no lack of light in Scripture. The problem is the "veil of darkness upon our hearts."[20] But God removes this veil so that we can discern "the mysteries" that are revealed in His Word.[21] As Manton explains, this removal is an involved process because there are multiple veils. There is "the veil of ignorance." We might understand God's truth literally and grammatically while remaining spiritually ignorant of it. This is akin to a child who reads the words in a story book without grasping their sense.[22] There is "the veil of carnal knowledge and wisdom." We possess a conceited opinion of ourselves—namely, our ability to understand and our assessment of how much we think we know. This arrogance keeps us from profiting from God's Word.[23] There is "the veil of prejudice and corrupt affections." Our attachment to this world

16. Manton, *Psalm 119*, 6:342.

17. Manton, *Psalm 119*, 6:360–61.

18. Manton, *Psalm 119*, 9:249. See John 6:45 and 1 Thess. 4:10.

19. Manton, *Psalm 119*, 6:116. See Ps. 36:9. Manton writes, "A man may see a truth rationally that doth not see it spiritually." He identifies four degrees of knowledge: simple nescience, grammatical knowledge, dogmatical knowledge, and gracious illumination. *Psalm 119*, 6:166. For more on illumination, see Thomas Manton, *Sermon on Philippians 3:15*, in Manton, *Works*, 2:75.

20. Manton, *Psalm 119*, 6:164. Of note, Manton observes, "When God is said to enlighten us, it is not that we should expect new revelations, but that we may see the wonders in his word, or get a clear sight of what is already revealed."

21. Manton, *Psalm 119*, 6:164. See also 6:353.

22. Manton, *Psalm 119*, 6:165. Acts 28:26.

23. Manton, *Psalm 119*, 6:165. See 1 Cor. 8:1–2.

inhibits us from discerning practical truths and from judging "the controversies of the age."[24] There is "the veil of carnal sense." We are shortsighted because we are so "inured to present things," which results in little appreciation for "things to come."[25] But, when God opens our eyes, He removes each of these veils.

In addition to removing the veils of ignorance, obstinacy, prejudice, and shortsightedness, God infuses light so that we obtain a clear discerning of "divine mysteries."[26] Our knowledge becomes lively to such a degree that it strengthens us against temptation, guards us from forgetfulness, and keeps divine truths ready at hand for our use.[27]

Inclination

"The understanding needs not only to be enlightened," writes Manton, "but the will to be moved and changed."[28] It is for this reason that the psalmist prays, "Incline my heart unto thy testimonies, and not to covetousness" (Ps. 119:36). The verb *incline* literally means to bend.[29] God inclines the heart when He bends it to that which is good.[30] We know this has happened "when the habitual bent of our affections is more to holiness than to worldly things; for the power of sin stands in the love of it, and so doth our aptness for grace in the love of it, or in the bent of the will, the strength of desire and affections by which we are carried out after it."[31] An inclined heart, therefore, is not a "simple

---

24. Manton, *Psalm 119*, 6:165. See 2 Peter 1:12.

25. Manton, *Psalm 119*, 6:165. See 2 Peter 1:9.

26. Manton, *Psalm 119*, 9:249.

27. "The Scriptures give no countenance to the notion that piety can exist without sound knowledge. The lamp of truth must light up our path to glory." Plumer, *Psalms*, 1025.

28. Manton, *Psalm 119*, 6:369.

29. "The inclining of the heart includes the enlightening of the mind, the inflaming of the affections and the liberating of the will—that is, the sanctification of the believer." Hywel Jones, *Psalm 119 for Life: Living Today in the Light of the Word* (Faverdale North, UK: EP Books, 2009), 58. Again, "The 'opening'…is a divine activity. It results in the wonders that are in the Word being displayed in such a way that they have an immense and lasting effect on the one whose mind is informed and whose heart is inflamed" (124).

30. Manton, *Psalm 119*, 6:371.

31. Manton, *Psalm 119*, 6:370.

approbation" of God's ways, nor is it a "bare wish."[32] Rather, it is a determination to obey God because we are swayed with love for God's commands. Manton explains, "You carry a sinning nature about with you; it is urging the heart to vanity, folly, and lust. So this will is present, urging the heart to good, and stirring up to holy motions."[33]

True Knowledge

God works powerfully when He teaches.[34] It is not only directive (illumination) but persuasive (inclination). "It is," says Manton, "effectual to alter and to change the affections, and to carry them out to Christ and to his ways."[35] This is a "very great gift," declares Manton.[36] When God teaches us, we know God's truth with greater clearness, certainty, and efficacy.[37] When we learn God's Word like this, it is deeply imprinted on our minds and hearts.[38] The result is communion with God, "for by knowing him, we come to enjoy him."[39]

For Manton, this constitutes true knowledge: "When God teaches, truth comes upon us with more conviction and demonstration (1 Corinthians 2:6), and so has a greater awe and sovereignty.... It does not only stay in the fancy, float in the brain, but affects the heart."[40] This conviction leads Manton to differentiate between "speculative" knowledge (i.e., "a bare notion of things") and "practical" knowledge.[41] He insists that there is a marked difference between knowing with the head (theoretical, notional, speculative knowledge) and knowing with the heart (practical, inclinational, sensible knowledge). That is to say, there is

---

32. Manton, *Psalm 119*, 8:151.

33. Manton, *Psalm 119*, 8:151.

34. Manton, *Psalm 119*, 8:347. Manton adds, "There is no way to the affections but by the ear, then to the understanding, and then passeth to the apprehension, the judgment, and conscience, and heart." *Psalm 119*, 7:439.

35. Manton, *Psalm 119*, 6:116. See also 6:52.

36. Manton, *Psalm 119*, 9:247.

37. Manton, *Psalm 119*, 9:252. See 1 Thess. 1:5.

38. Manton, *Psalm 119*, 6:167.

39. Manton, *Psalm 119*, 9:251.

40. Manton, *Psalm 119*, 6:118.

41. See *Psalm 119*, 6:51–52, 65–67, 256–58, 341–42; 7:271–73; 8:279–80; 9:32–33.

a significant difference between *thinking* that honey is sweet and *tasting* that honey is sweet. In short, practical knowledge is "operative," meaning it produces "a change both in the inward and outward man" whereby our practice is brought into greater conformity with God's Word.[42]

When the psalmist prays for knowledge and understanding, he is not asking for the speculative, but the practical. He wants to learn how to walk in God's ways. Likewise, all the teaching that we receive from God must be directed to practice.[43] "This is God's intention in teaching," says Manton, "therefore it should be our end in learning."[44]

Conclusion

"Let my heart be sound in thy statutes; that I be not ashamed" (Ps. 119:80). According to Manton, we possess a sound heart when God's Word is rooted to such a degree that it "diffuseth its influence for the seasoning of every affection, and beareth a universal sovereignty over us."[45] For a description of this, he turns to James 1:21, "Wherefore lay apart all filthiness and superfluity of naughtiness, and receive with meekness the engrafted word, which is able to save your souls." We have received God's Word only when it has become a part of us: "Thy words were found, and I did eat them; and thy word was unto me the joy and rejoicing of mine heart" (Jer. 15:16).[46] This eating includes "an enlightened understanding," "an awakened conscience," "a rightly disposed will," and "purged and quickened affections."[47] Of particular significance is Manton's contention that "God doth not write his law upon our hearts by enthusiasm, rapture, and inspiration, as he wrote in the hearts of the apostles and prophets, but maketh use of our reason, reading, hearing, meditation, conference, and prayer." Our constant prayer, therefore, is for God to teach us His Word.[48]

---

42. Manton, *Psalm 119*, 7:271.
43. Manton, *Psalm 119*, 6:346.
44. Manton, *Psalm 119*, 6:346.
45. Manton, *Psalm 119*, 7:341.
46. Manton, *Psalm 119*, 7:341. See Heb. 8:10.
47. Manton, *Psalm 119*, 7:342–43.
48. Manton, *Psalm 119*, 7:433.

Chapter 7

The Increase of Blessedness

As discussed in the previous chapter, true knowledge, for Manton, is practical. It is learning how to walk in God's ways. This conformity to God's will is essential to blessedness. As Manton explains in his fifth proposition, "The more we are brought to attend upon the word, and the more influence the word has upon us, the nearer the blessing."[1] Manton's reasoning is simple. As God instructs us through His Word, we are conformed to His nature, meaning "we love what he loves, and hate what he hates."[2] As we become more like Him, we naturally grow in our enjoyment of Him.[3] Manton develops this premise in his opening sermons on Psalm 119.[4]

The Course of Our Life

God's Word dictates, first, the course of our life: "Blessed are the undefiled in the way, who walk in the law of the LORD" (Ps. 119:1).[5] Here

---

1. Manton, *Psalm 119*, 6:113. This proposition is derived from Prov. 8:34 and Acts 8:36.

2. Manton, *Psalm 119*, 6:110.

3. Manton remarks, "Let it be your care, then, to drive on the great design of holiness; this will conform you to God, which is man's excellency; bring you to enjoy God, which is man's happiness (Matthew 5:8; Hebrews 12:14)." *Exposition of James*, 4:313.

4. "These eight verses teach that true piety is sincere, consistent, practical, hearty, intelligent, earnest, active, stirring, diligent, humble, distrustful of itself, symmetrical, guileless, unspotted from the world, self-renouncing, confident in God, delighting in thankfulness, fully prepared to keep the law, and as ready to confess that without divine grace it can do nothing." Plumer, *Psalms*, 1025.

5. Manton, *Psalm 119*, 6:15, 38. "The general scope and design of it is to magnify

the psalmist describes how the blessed walk (they are "undefiled in the way") and where the blessed walk ("in the law of the LORD"). From this Manton concludes that the only way to true blessedness is found in "sincere, constant, uniform obedience to God's law."[6] Such obedience means endeavoring to "approve" ourselves to God.[7]

Manton is careful to note that there is a twofold obedience in Scripture: (1) legal, which is perfect conformity to God's will, and (2) gospel (or evangelical), which is sincerity in seeking to obey God's will.[8] "This sincere obedience," says Manton, "is known by our endeavors after perfection, and our repentance for defects." He adds, "Where there is a general purpose to please God, and a hearty sorrow when we offend him, this is the sincerity which the gospel accepteth of."[9]

Manton's understanding of evangelical obedience must be set in the context of his covenant theology. He speaks of two covenants, the first of which is the covenant of works.[10] In the garden of Eden, Adam stood in the place of his descendants, so when he rebelled against the specific commandment God gave him, God counted his sin as his posterity's sin, his guilt as his posterity's guilt, and his punishment as his posterity's punishment. For this reason, there was a need for another covenant—the covenant of grace, whereby God commands us to receive Christ through faith. This means that Adam has

---

the law, and make it honorable; to set forth the excellency and usefulness of divine revelation, and to recommend it to us for the government of ourselves." Henry, *Commentary on the Whole Bible*, 705. "There are two things which the prophet mainly aims at: the exhorting of the children of God to follow godliness and a holy life; and the prescribing of the rule, and pointing out the form of the true worship of God, so that the faithful may devote themselves wholly to the study of the law." Calvin, *Commentary on the Book of Psalms*, 4:398.

6. Manton, *Psalm 119*, 6:9.

7. Manton, *Psalm 119*, 6:11.

8. Manton, *Psalm 119*, 6:20. See also 6:357; 7:96–97; 9:223. Manton also explains this distinction in *Sermon on Philippians 3:15*, 2:58–62.

9. Manton, *Psalm 119*, 6:20. We obey God's commandments according to "the terms of grace" that He offers in Christ: He grants pardon and accepts repentance. *Psalm 119*, 9:223.

10. Manton, *Psalm 119*, 7:319.

a counterpart—the last Adam (Christ).[11] Adam disobeyed ("by one man's disobedience many were made sinners"), whereas Christ obeyed ("by the obedience of one shall many be made righteous") (Rom. 5:19). We are no longer in Adam (under the covenant of works), because we have been united with Christ (under the covenant of grace), who has fulfilled the covenant of works on our behalf.

With this paradigm in place, Manton maintains that the law functions as both "a covenant of works" and "a rule of life." As it is a covenant of works, Christ has fulfilled it on behalf of those who have an interest in Him. As it is a rule of life under the new covenant, "we give up ourselves to God to walk according to the tenor of it."[12] Under the new covenant, God accepts our "single-hearted inclination" to observe His will, while ensuring that Christ's "perfect righteousness" covers our "defects and weaknesses."[13]

The Frame of Our Heart

God's Word dictates, second, the frame of our heart: "Blessed are they that keep his testimonies, and that seek him with the whole heart" (Ps. 119:2).[14] Manton sees two features of the blessed man in this verse. The first is what he *keeps*: God's testimonies. This keeping of God's Word is possible because God enlightens our minds to understand His will and frames our affections to obey His will. Manton concludes, "So long as we bewail sin, seek remission of sin, strive after perfection, endeavor to keep close and be tender of a command, though a naughty heart will carry us aside sometimes, we keep the testimony of the Lord in a gospel sense."[15]

---

11. See Manton, *Temptation of Christ*, 1:261–62.

12. Manton, *Psalm 119*, 7:221.

13. Manton, *Psalm 119*, 9:223. For Manton's repudiation of libertinism, see *Exposition of Jude*, 5:6–7, 102–3, 114–15, 123, 148–49, 151, 175, 235–36, 270, 277, 284, 300, 312, 318, 320, 325, 334, 360. He rebukes the libertines for their looseness, laziness, and licentiousness. *Exposition of Jude*, 5:146.

14. Manton, *Psalm 119*, 6:15, 38. For "whole heart," see Ps. 119:2, 10, 34.

15. Manton, *Psalm 119*, 6:20.

The second feature of the blessed man is what he *seeks*: he seeks God with his whole heart. We seek God by way of reconciliation because we were alienated from Him at the time of Adam's fall. We also seek God by way of supply because we encounter innumerable troubles in this fallen world. The psalmist is not speaking of either of these but of our seeking communion with God in His ordinances.[16] God stirs our faith, hope, and love as we seek Him in the means He has appointed for our spiritual nourishment. For this reason, Manton exhorts his listeners to seek God early, daily, and tirelessly.[17] He warns, "There are many that hover about the palace, that yet do not speak with the prince; so possibly we may hover about ordinances, and not meet with God there."[18]

According to Manton, the whole heart denotes "extension of parts" (the mind, affections, and will) and "intension of degrees" (the highest elevation of our hearts).[19] If we give only a part to God, we really give Him nothing, "for that part that is reserved will in time draw the whole after him."[20] Again, Manton is adamant that we are not to understand this pursuit of God in "the legal sense with respect to absolute perfection" but rather in a gospel (or evangelical) sense, meaning we are to use "all good means to cleave to God," repent of "our defects…with kindly remorse," and seek "pardon and peace in Christ's name."[21] Manton's

---

16. Manton, *Psalm 119*, 6:20.

17. Manton is quick to note that we do these things only in Christ by "the help of his own Spirit." *Psalm 119*, 6:25.

18. Manton, *Psalm 119*, 6:22.

19. Manton, *Psalm 119*, 6:26–27. Elsewhere Manton says that to seek God with "the whole heart" is to seek Him with "sincerity of aims," "integrity of parts," and "uniformity of endeavors." *Psalm 119*, 6:94.

20. Manton, *Psalm 119*, 6:357. Manton declares, "God will have all or nothing." *Psalm 119*, 6:359. Who are those who fail to give their whole heart to God? Those who are "for God in their consciences but not in their affections"; those who have affections "divided between God and the world"; and those who do "many things, but stick at one point of their duty to God." *Psalm 119*, 6:359.

21. Manton, *Psalm 119*, 6:27–29. Manton writes, "When God sanctifieth a man he sanctifieth him as to all parts and faculties of body and soul, enlighteneth the understanding with the knowledge of his will, inclineth the heart to obedience, circumciseth the affection, filleth us with the love of God himself and holy things. But being a voluntary agent, he doth not this as to perfection of degrees all at once, but successively, and by little and little. Therefore, as long as we are in the world there is somewhat of

point is that the blessed man no longer sins by way of course. "We might fall into the dirt," says he, "but we do not wallow in it like swine in the mire."[22]

The Integrity of Our Obedience

God's Word dictates, third, the integrity of our obedience: "They also do no iniquity: they walk in his ways" (Ps. 119:3).[23] Having considered holiness in terms of its subject (the life of man in Ps. 119:1) and object (the heart of man in Ps. 119:2), Manton now turns to its expression, which consists of two parts.

The first is negative: there is "an eschewing of sin" in that the blessed "do no iniquity."[24] How is this possible? The answer is that the psalmist has in view those to whom God "imputeth no sin" because they "are renewed by grace, and reconciled to God by Christ Jesus."[25] Because of their new identity in Christ, they make it their business to avoid sin: they sin not with the whole heart but with the "dislike and reluctance of the new nature"; they do not sin by way of course, meaning it is not easy, constant, or frequent to them; they do not rest in sin, in that "they do not lie and wallow there like swine in the mire"; and they struggle against sin, groaning under its "relics."[26] When we make it our business to avoid sin in this manner, we are blessed: "As sin is taken away, so our happiness increaseth."[27]

The second expression of holiness is positive: there is "a studying to please God" in that the blessed "walk in his ways." Simply put, our

---

ignorance in the understanding, perversity in the will, fleshliness and impurity in the affections, flesh and spirit in every faculty, like water and wine in the same cup." *Psalm 119*, 6:357.

22. Manton, *Psalm 119*, 6:34.

23. Manton, *Psalm 119*, 6:38. Manton believes that Ps. 119:3 is cited in James 1:25. "It is an argument, or evidence of our blessedness, though not the ground of it; the way, though not the cause." *Exposition of James*, 4:162.

24. Manton, *Psalm 119*, 6:29. Manton provides a detailed explanation of what it means to hate sin in *Psalm 119*, 8:56–63.

25. Manton, *Psalm 119*, 6:30.

26. Manton, *Psalm 119*, 6:33–34.

27. Manton, *Psalm 119*, 6:32.

desire is not only to avoid evil but to do good.[28] We arm ourselves with a resolution to obey God's will, even if it is contrary to our own.[29] We receive God's commands with due reverence, recognizing that they are "holy, and just, and good" (Rom. 7:12). Manton comments, "There is a ready willing heart to obey them and conform to them in the regenerate, therefore an assent is not enough, but a consent; this is that they would choose and prefer before liberty; they acquiesce and are satisfied in their rule as the best rule for them to live by."[30]

Conclusion

"And I will walk at liberty: for I seek thy precepts" (Ps. 119:45). Most people are convinced that freedom is doing whatever they please. For Manton, however, liberty "is not a power to live as we list" but "to live as we ought."[31] Anything that hinders us from pursuing our great end, which is to be happy in God, robs us of freedom.[32] "True liberty," therefore, "is in the ways of God" when we discover "how to attain to our great end, which is true blessedness."[33]

---

28. Manton, *Psalm 119*, 6:37.

29. Manton, *Psalm 119*, 7:219. Manton adds, "Many of the commandments are crossing to our natural inclinations and corrupt humors, or contrary to our interests in the world, our profit, pleasure; and nothing will hold the heart to our duty but the conscience of God's authority." *Psalm 119*, 7:219–20.

30. Manton, *Psalm 119*, 7:215.

31. Manton, *Psalm 119*, 6:479. Elsewhere Manton writes, "Duty is the greatest liberty, and sin the greatest bondage." *Exposition of James*, 4:164.

32. Manton develops this as follows: (1) "That infringeth a man's liberty that hindereth and disableth him from prosecuting his great end, which is to be truly happy." (2) "That which disordereth the constitution of the soul, and puts reason out of dominion, that certainly is spiritual bondage and thralldom." (3) "Consider the great tyranny and power of sin; it leaveth us no right and power to dispose of ourselves and our actions, and so men cannot help themselves when they would." (4) "Consider how this bondage is always increased by custom, which is a second nature, or an inveterate disease not easily cured." (5) "The fear of death and terror which doth arise from the consciousness of sin, the fear of death and damnation, and wrath to come, which doggeth sin at the heels." *Psalm 119*, 6:480–82.

33. Manton, *Psalm 119*, 6:482. "We are here informed that true wisdom consists in being wise according to the law of God, that it may preserve us in fear and obedience to him." Calvin, *Commentary on the Book of Psalms*, 4:425. "The spirit of true piety is

This liberty frees us from those "unquiet thoughts" that haunt the disobedient. "Look," exhorts Manton, "as cheerfulness and liveliness accompanieth perfect health…so this serenity and quiet in the soul, the regular and orderly motion of our faculties; there is a sweet contentment of mind resulting from it."[34] Liberty also leads to "gracious experiences and manifestations of God."[35] Christ declares, "He that hath my commandments, and keepeth them, he it is that loveth me: and he that loveth me shall be loved of my Father, and I will love him, and will manifest myself to him" (John 14:21). Again, He declares, "If ye keep my commandments, ye shall abide in my love" (John 15:10). This abiding in God's love entails a dwelling sense of God's love on the heart whereby we are "taken into sweet fellowship and communion with God."[36] It is contingent on obedience. For Manton, therefore, the means to blessedness is a life conformed to and a heart committed to God's Word.

---

one of steadfast obedience, and of perseverance in the ways of God." Plumer, *Psalms*, 1037. Again, "It is a part of true piety to seek to know as well as to keep the divine precepts," *Psalms*, 1041. "Obedience to the Lord's will is…the hallmark of true piety." Jones, *Psalm 119 for Life*, 30.

34. Manton, *Psalm 119*, 7:98. See Rom. 5:11; 14:17; Gal. 6:16.
35. Manton, *Psalm 119*, 7:100.
36. Manton, *Psalm 119*, 7:100.

Chapter 8

The Focus of Blessedness

Manton's final proposition concerning the way to the enjoyment of God's blessedness is as follows: "It is not only an affront put upon God, but also a great wrong, to neglect the word of God, and the way he prescribes, and to seek blessedness in temporal things."[1] Manton is adamant that temporal things cannot provide us with true blessedness: they cannot fill the heart because they are finite in nature; they cannot reach the heart because they are material in nature; and they cannot satisfy the heart because they are temporal in nature. "Nothing can give us solid peace," affirms Manton, "but what doth make us eternally happy."[2] This means that we can never know blessedness apart from "the infinite God." Any attempt to find it elsewhere is an exercise in futility.

Manton develops this proposition in his sermon on Psalm 119:36, in which the psalmist prays, "Incline my heart unto thy testimonies, and not to covetousness." Manton begins his exposition by explaining that our heart is inclined to something—that is to say, it always looks to something outside of itself to satisfy it.[3] It is like a sponge, which sucks in moisture from other things. As Manton puts it, our heart is "a chaos of desires, seeking to be filled with something from without."[4] Because the heart is destitute of God's grace, it looks to temporal things to provide satisfaction. God created us in His image, but we lost

---

1. Manton, *Psalm 119*, 6:113. This proposition is derived from Ps. 16:11.
2. Manton, *Psalm 119*, 6:7–8.
3. Manton, *Psalm 119*, 6:372.
4. Manton, *Psalm 119*, 6:372.

original righteousness at the time of Adam's fall. As a result, our heart
has lost all appreciation for the spiritual and eternal, moving instead
toward the material and temporal—namely, the pleasures of the body.

In this condition, we cannot incline ourselves toward "that which
is spiritual and heavenly," because we have no taste for it.[5] Manton
declares, "There is no principle remaining in us that can alter this
frame, or make us so far unsatisfied with our present state as to look
after other things, that can break the force of our natural and cus-
tomary inclinations."[6] This being the case, God must renew our heart
before we will look to Him as "our last end and our chiefest good."[7]
This renewal involves the weakening of the old inclination to "carnal
vanities" and the implantation of "a new bent."[8] But it does not involve
the complete eradication of the old inclination. We are still "apt to
return to the old bent and bias," for there are "some relics of our natural
averseness from God."[9] For this reason we stand in need of continual
renewal, hence the psalmist's prayer: "Incline my heart unto thy testimonies, and not to covetousness."

The Affections

Manton's concept of renewal as the weakening of the heart's inclination
to the material and temporal as its chief end and the strengthening of
the heart's inclination to the spiritual and eternal (namely, the blessed
God) as its chief end is rooted in his understanding of the affections.
He maintains that the soul consists of faculties that should command
and direct (understanding, affections, will), and faculties that should
be commanded and directed (phantasy, appetite, sense).[10] By God's

5. Manton, *Psalm 119*, 6:374.
6. Manton, *Psalm 119*, 6:375.
7. Manton, *Psalm 119*, 6:373.
8. Manton, *Psalm 119*, 6:376.
9. Manton, *Psalm 119*, 6:377.
10. Manton, *Psalm 119*, 9:304. Manton holds to a bipartite view of man—he is
body and soul. See, for example, *Sermon on Ecclesiastes 12:7*, in Manton, *Works*, 19:61–
64. Some texts of Scripture seem to indicate that we are tripartite in nature: body, soul,
and spirit (Matt. 22:37; 1 Thess. 5:23; Heb. 4:12). According to this view, the soul is the
seat of self-consciousness, whereas the spirit is the seat of God-consciousness. Manton

design, our understanding is supposed to counsel and command our affections. These, in turn, are supposed to move our phantasy (or imagination), which then controls our senses and the members of our body.[11] As a result of the fall, however, this order has been corrupted. The commanding faculties are now "blind and sleepy," while the commanded faculties are now "obstinate" and "rebellious."[12] This means that bodily pleasure now affects the senses; the senses move the phantasy; the phantasy controls the affections; and the affections blind the mind and captivate the will. As a result of this corruption, we are "carried headlong" to destruction.[13] Manton summarizes, "Hence it is that all our faculties are perverted, the mind is become blind and vain, the will stubborn and perverse, conscience stupid, the affections preoccupied and entangled, and we find a manifest disproportion in all our faculties to things carnal and spiritual, sinful and holy."[14]

In terms of the soul's faculties, the affections are of paramount importance, for they are "the forcible and vigorous motions of the will."[15] Manton adds, "A man is never truly converted to God till God

---

disagrees. He believes the terms *soul* and *spirit* are used to note "the theological distinction of the faculties." *Exposition of Jude*, 5:28. It is worth noting that, in Scripture, the expressions *body and soul* and *body and spirit* are used to refer to the whole person (Matt. 10:28; 1 Cor. 7:34; 2 Cor. 7:1; James 2:26). Plus, the terms *soul* and *spirit* are used interchangeably. Grief and sorrow are experienced in both (1 Kings 21:5; Ps. 42:11; Matt. 26:38; Mark 8:12; John 12:27; 13:21; Acts 17:16; 2 Peter 2:8). Joy and spiritual desire are experienced in both (Pss. 42:1–5; 63:3; 103:1–2; 116:7; 130:6; Isa. 26:9; Luke 1:46–47). Devotion to God is experienced in both (Mark 12:30; Acts 4:32; 14:22; Eph. 6:6; Phil. 1:27).

11. Manton, *Psalm 119*, 9:305–6.

12. Manton, *Psalm 119*, 9:304, 305.

13. Manton, *Psalm 119*, 9:306. He adds, "Our affections are so apt to be led by sense and not by right reason, that there is many times great danger that in seeing we should not see, lest seeing, knowing, and approving that which is better, we should embrace and follow that which is worse and act contrary to our knowledge and conscience." *Psalm 119*, 9:308–9.

14. Manton, *Psalm 119*, 7:273.

15. Manton, *Psalm 119*, 6:358. Manton adds, "Man findeth a force within himself, his heart maketh him willing; the stronger the affections, the better the man acteth, with greater strength and vivacity; for they are the vigorous motions of the will." *Psalm 119*, 8:359.

hath his love, and his law hath his love; for the constitution of the heart is not seen in our opinions so much as in our affections, love, desire, and delight. Many men's judgment is for God; that is, conscience is for God, but their hearts are for other things."[16] This implies that the battle for the soul is the battle for the affections. Manton inherits this view from Augustine, who identified four primary "motions" of the will: desire, delight (or joy), fear, and sorrow.[17] Desire and delight are the "volition of consent" to a loved object: desire occurs when consent takes the form of seeking the object, and delight occurs when consent takes the form of enjoying it. On the other hand, fear and sorrow are the "volition of aversion" from a hated object: fear occurs when aversion takes the form of turning from the object, and sorrow occurs when aversion takes the form of experiencing it.[18]

In this paradigm, love and hate ultimately determine the response of the other affections: desire is yearning for what is loved; delight is experiencing what is loved; fear is fleeing from what is hated; and sorrow is experiencing what is hated. From this, Augustine argued that as long as the object of our love is "well-directed," the affections are good. This changes, of course, if the object of our love is "ill-directed."[19] Prior to Adam's fall, the object of man's love was God and, as a result, the affections were good. This condition, however, was terminated at the time of the fall when love for God was lost and, consequently, the affections became evil. At regeneration, our love is again well directed, and the affections respond accordingly.[20] Augustine summarizes, "The citizens of the holy city of God, who live according to God in the pilgrimage of this life, both fear and desire, and grieve and rejoice.

16. Manton, *Psalm 119*, 7:317.

17. Augustine, *The City of God*, in *A Select Library of the Nicene and Post-Nicene Fathers of the Christian Church*, vol. 2, ed. P. Schaff (New York: Random House, 1948), 14.5.

18. Augustine, *City of God* 14.6.

19. Augustine, *City of God* 14.7.

20. Because we perceive God's goodness in creation, providence, and redemption, we take Him as our blessedness. This is evident in "a desire after him" and "a delight in him." Manton, *Sermons on Romans 8*, 12:278.

And because their love is rightly placed, all these affections of theirs are right."[21]

Manton adopts Augustine's paradigm, affirming that the affections are the inclination or disinclination of the soul to an object in accordance with the soul's perception of that object as either desirous or odious.[22] "Love is the great wheel of the soul, that sets all a-going," declares Manton.[23] It is a complacency in and a propensity toward whatever the soul perceives to be good; it expresses itself in desire in the absence of the good, and delight in the presence of the good.[24] "Of all affections," explains Manton, "desires are most earnest and vehement, for they are the vigorous bent of the heart to that which is good…. This affection of union, simply considered, is love, which is an inclination of the soul to good, it presseth the heart to it; but as it is an absent good, it is desire, which exciteth to pursue it earnestly."[25]

Prior to the fall, the affections were well directed because love ("the great wheel of the soul") was set on God. In man's fallen condition, however, the affections are ill directed because love is set on self.[26] "We have the same affections," says Manton, "but they are misplaced; we

---

21. Augustine, *City of God* 14.9. "The fall of man has misplaced his affections. Love was originally made for God and His law;—hatred, for sin. Now man loves what he ought to hate (John 3:19; Romans 1:32; 6:12), and hates what he ought to love (Job 21:14; Psalm 14:1; Romans 8:7). The work of divine grace is to restore the disordered affections to their proper center, and to bestow them on the right object;—hating vain thoughts, and loving the law of God." Bridges, *Psalm 119*, 284.

22. Manton writes, "Affection against affection, hatred against love. Love and hatred are natural affections, which are good or evil according to the objects to which they are applied…. Set them upon their proper objects, and they express a gracious constitution of soul…. Man needeth affections of aversation as well as choice and pursuit. Hatred hath its use as well as love." *Psalm 119*, 9:180.

23. Manton, *Psalm 119*, 8:156. Manton comments, "Since there are two competitors for the heart of man, and his love cannot lie idle, it must be given to one or another; love and oblectation cannot remain idle in the soul, either it must leak out to the world, or run out to God." *Psalm 119*, 9:268.

24. Manton, *Psalm 119*, 9:20–21. See also 7:7.

25. Manton, *Psalm 119*, 8:359.

26. Manton notes, "That self which we must hate or deny is that self which stands in opposition to God or competition with him, and so jostleth with him for the throne." *A Treatise of Self-Denial*, in Manton, *Works*, 15:182.

love where we should hate, and hate where we should love." Our affections, therefore, are like "a member out of joint."[27]

The Practice of Moderation

All of this is important for making sense of Manton's sixth proposition: "It is not only an affront put upon God, but also a great wrong, to neglect the word of God, and the way he prescribes, and to seek blessedness in temporal things." Because of our disordered affections, this is precisely what we do. Even in a regenerate state, we struggle with ill-directed love. Manton writes, "The heart of man standeth between two objects—the laws of God and carnal vanities. In our natural estate we are wholly bent to please the flesh; in our renewed estate there is a new bent put upon the heart. Now the old bent is not wholly gone, though overmastered and overpowered: the false bias of corruption will still incline us to the delights of sense; but the new bias to the way everlasting, to spiritual eternal happiness: as that prevaileth, we love and delight in the commandments of God."[28] Given our condition, we must pursue moderation.[29]

Manton has no difficulty with the affections: "Some have vainly thought affections to be an after-growth of noisome weeds in our nature corrupted; whereas they are wholesome herbs, implanted in us by God at our first creation, of great use to grace when rightly stirred and ordered."[30] For that matter, neither does Manton have any difficulty with strong affections as long as they are well directed.[31] When they are, they are moderated in terms of their attachment to earthly things.

---

27. Manton, *Psalm 119*, 8:155.

28. Manton, *Psalm 119*, 7:9.

29. Manton is no Stoic. The Stoics believed that everyone possesses impulses—inclinations toward or away from objects. While reason is in control, these impulses are not an issue. However, when they exceed the bounds of reason, they become passions: fear, sorrow, pleasure, and desire. The external factors that cause these passions are without virtue; thus, the passions themselves are irrational. Virtue then is a state of moderation attained when people become indifferent toward externals, thereby freeing themselves from passions.

30. Manton, *Psalm 119*, 8:230.

31. Manton, *Exposition of James*, 4:306. George Swinnock explains, "According

According to Manton, there are two appetites: sensitive and rational.[32] Sensitive love is the "complacency of the sensitive appetite" in whatever the senses deem good, whereas rational love is the "complacency of the rational appetite" in whatever reason deems good. Self-love is the love of happiness. In innocence, the soul is directed by a true self-love.[33] It loves happiness. With its rational appetite, it views God as the greatest good. It loves God and, therefore, its affections are well directed. In this state, the soul's sensitive appetite follows the lead of its rational appetite, meaning its love for the creature is moderated by its love for God. In apostasy, the soul is directed by a false self-love.[34] It still loves happiness. The problem, however, is that man no longer views God as the greatest good. The soul no longer loves God and, therefore, its affections are ill directed. In this state, the soul's sensitive appetite no longer follows the lead of its rational appetite, meaning its love for the creature is no longer moderated by its love for God. As a matter of fact, the rational appetite has fallen under the control of the sensitive appetite. As a result, man seeks to be happy according to his "carnal

---

to the price we set upon things, such is our pleasure and joy in their presence, and our pain and sorrow in their absence." This mention of the four passions is followed by an exhortation to prepare for adversity: "Love heaven as thy paradise, and look on earth but as the place of thy pilgrimage, then thou wilt cheerfully travel in all ways, whether fair or foul." In all this, Swinnock never suggests that the four passions are irrational. He encourages the subjection of the passions to reason because they are set on the wrong object—earth. It is this misdirection that makes them excessive. If people love heaven as their paradise, there is no immoderation. *Works of George Swinnock*, 2:72–73.

32. For more on this, see John Flavel, *Pneumatologia: A Treatise on the Soul of Man*, in *Works of John Flavel*, 2:493; and John Bunyan, *The Greatness of the Soul, and Unspeakableness of the Loss Thereof, &c.*, in *The Miscellaneous Works of John Bunyan* (Oxford: Clarendon Press, 1981), 9:144.

33. A century later, Jonathan Edwards articulates the same concept of self-love. For a summary of his position, see *Charity and Its Fruits: Christian Love as Manifested in the Heart and Life* (1852; repr., Edinburgh: Banner of Truth, 2000), 157–66.

34. Manton identifies a fourfold self-love: carnal, natural, spiritual, and glorified. See *Practical Exposition of the Lord's Prayer*, in Manton, *Works*, 1:67–69. Charnock describes a threefold self-love: *natural*, a desire to seek our good; *carnal*, a desire to be superior to God; and *gracious*, a desire to fulfill our end, that is, to glorify God. *Existence and Attributes of God*, 1:136.

fancies."[35] He makes himself as happy as he can "in the enjoyment of present things."[36] "All sin is but carnal self-love," declares Manton.[37] In renewal, true self-love is restored—at least, in part. This means the affections are caught between the sensitive and rational appetites. In this state, our goal is to gain mastery over the sensitive appetite. Earthly things have a tremendous influence on our affections because they are "sensible and near." By our senses, they "obtrude and thrust themselves upon the soul."[38] For this reason, we exercise moderation: the inclination of our hearts to God's testimonies and not to covetousness.

Manton has no problem in deriving pleasure from the created order. God created all things and declared all things to be good. Earthly things are "good in themselves, and that self-love which carrieth us out to them is naturally good."[39] This good becomes evil, however, when our love of these things usurps our love of God. The way to holiness, therefore, is not found in abstaining from God's good gifts but in carefully enjoying them.[40] We must not overvalue natural delights according to our sinful inclination; rather, we must moderate our use

---

35. Manton, *Psalm 119*, 6:7. Manton states elsewhere, "By the change of our end all moral goodness is lost, for all means are subordinate to the last end, and are determined by it. Now necessarily thus it will be without grace; there will be a conversion of a man to the creature and the body, with the conveniences and comforts thereof; the interest and concernments of the body are set up instead of God." *Psalm 119*, 6:373.

36. Manton, *Psalm 119*, 6:7.

37. Manton, *Sermon on Ecclesiastes 7:29*, 19:56.

38. Manton, *Psalm 119*, 8:362–63.

39. Manton, *Psalm 119*, 6:372–73.

40. It is worth noting, therefore, that Manton is no ascetic. Ascetical theology is concerned with the means of attaining Christian perfection. All that belongs to the material realm inhibits the pursuit of union with God; therefore, it is sin. As such, we are to mortify it. Throughout their history, both the Roman Catholic Church (in the West) and the Orthodox Church (in the East) have developed elaborate systems of asceticism. Underpinning these systems is the belief in the threefold path to God: purification, contemplation, and union. The goal of the spiritual life is to arrive at a state of impassibility, whereby we are no longer affected by the external world. When we reach this passionless state, we engage in contemplative (wordless) prayer in which we lay our hearts open before God in silence. This leads to a constant experience of the divine reality. This is best achieved in isolation from others. In other words, it is not a corporate pursuit.

of them according to the fear of God.[41] The issue is not food, drink, or any other delight. Manton has no qualms with such outward pleasures. They are good because God ordained them. The issue is covetousness, whereby the soul seeks its satisfaction in these things apart from God.[42]

Conclusion

For Manton, our greatest desire should be to know God as revealed in His Word: "As we are to love God, so in proportion his word, which is the means to enjoy him; therefore here we should stretch our desire to the utmost."[43] We look into God's Word "with an eye of love," and the more we see His loveliness, the more we desire Him.[44] It is impossible to hide this kind of affection. "If there be longing, there will be fainting, gasping, breathing; for strong desires are hasty and impatient of satisfaction."[45] How do we kindle such desire? The answer, for Manton, is simple: "Mortify and moderate your affections to the world and worldly things, and meddle sparingly with the comforts thereof; otherwise your hearts will be apt immoderately to leak out after them, to the interruption of the spiritual life."[46]

---

41. For Manton's approach to earthly delights (e.g., food, apparel, recreation), see *Sermons on Titus 2:11–14*, 16:118–42.

42. The Bible is not opposed to human experience, but human experience that is sinful. See Gal. 5:19–21 for a definition of the flesh. Sin is never confused with the physical, even though at times it touches the physical. The Bible singles out two dangers: materialism and selfishness. At times, we deny self to suffer with Christ (Matt. 10:34; 16:24–25; Acts 14:21–22; 1 Cor. 4:11–12; Phil. 1:29; Heb. 10:32). At times, we deny self to proclaim the gospel (Phil. 2:5–7; Col. 1:24–29). We are prepared to deny "natural" delight—not because we despise the material world (including life) but because we see a deeper significance to life than mere physical existence. For Manton's concept of self-denial, see *Treatise on Self-Denial*, 15:175–294, which is an exposition of Matt. 16:24.

43. Manton, *Psalm 119*, 8:360.

44. Manton, *Psalm 119*, 8:361.

45. Manton, *Psalm 119*, 8:360.

46. Manton, *Psalm 119*, 8:365.

Chapter 9

The Sufficiency of Scripture

The previous six chapters have demonstrated how Manton believes we come to the enjoyment of God—our "chiefest good" and "utmost end."[1] In sum, God impresses His excellencies on us through His Word, thereby stirring our affections so that we make returns to Him—faith, love, humility, and repentance. God's Word, therefore, stands at the center of Manton's spirituality. It alone is the means through which God speaks to us and we respond to Him.[2]

Manton's convictions concerning the sufficiency of Scripture are on full display in the propositions he derives from Paul's admonition in 2 Thessalonians 2:15, "Therefore, brethren, stand fast, and hold the traditions which ye have been taught, whether by word, or our epistle."[3] Manton's first proposition is that "whatever assurance we have of God's preserving us in the truth, yet we are bound to use diligence

---

1. Manton, *Psalm 119*, 6:108. For more on God as the "first cause," "chief good," "supreme truth," and "utmost end," see *Exposition of Jude*, 5:136–42.

2. How do we know God has revealed the Scriptures? (1) "Partly because these writings are delivered to us by the universal tradition of the church." (2) "Partly because of the consent between the prophets and the apostles, the one foretelling whatever the other declared as accomplished." (3) "Partly because the doctrines have an impress of God upon them…[they] become his wisdom…holiness…and power." (4) "Partly because it agreeth with the nature of man, so far as a man hath any good left in him. It agreeth with the necessities of man, his guilty fears and his desires of happiness." (5) "Partly because God hath witnessed and attested it by his Spirit." Manton concludes, "Upon these accounts we receive what is written in the prophets and apostles as revealed by God." *Sermons on Acts 24:14–16*, in Manton, *Works*, 17:420–21.

3. For a similar treatment, see *Exposition of Jude*, 5:107–12, 322–24.

and caution."[4] This is implied in Paul's command: "Therefore, brethren, stand fast." Manton points out that the expression "stand fast" describes a soldier who keeps his ground amid the battle. In his next proposition he states, "The means of standing fast is by holding the traditions which were taught by the holy apostles."[5] The gospel is not man's invention, but God's revelation, in that Christ manifested it to His "chosen witnesses," who then shared it with others.[6] In this sense, it is a "tradition, or a delivery of the truth upon the testimony of one that came from God to instruct the world."[7] We stand fast by holding to this tradition.

Building on these two propositions, Manton adds another: "That whilst the apostles were in being, there were two ways of delivering the truth, and that was by word of mouth and writing."[8] At first, the apostles proclaimed what they had received from Christ; then, they "consigned it to writing for the use of all ages." In this way, they sanctioned the canon of the New Testament. Manton's final proposition is the most significant for the present discussion: "That now, when they are long since gone to God, and we cannot receive from them the doctrine of life by word of mouth, we must stick to the Scriptures or written word."[9] Recognizing the frailty of man's memory, the apostles ensured that an authentic record would remain, after their departure, by which our "joy may be full" (1 John 1:4). This joy is discovered in

---

4. Thomas Manton, *Scripture Sufficient without Unwritten Traditions*, in Manton, *Works*, 5:488.

5. Manton, *Scripture Sufficient*, 5:490.

6. See 2 Tim. 2:2; Heb. 2:3–4.

7. Manton, *Scripture Sufficient*, 5:491.

8. Manton, *Scripture Sufficient*, 5:494.

9. Manton, *Scripture Sufficient*, 5:494. Manton contends that Christ and His apostles teach us to stick to the written Word by their constant appeal to the Old Testament Scriptures as their authority (Matt. 15:2; Luke 16:31; Acts 26:22). He also asserts that we must follow Peter who tells us that we have "a more sure word of prophecy" to which we must pay attention (2 Peter 1:19). He remarks, "Law and prophets is an expression commonly used for all the scriptures extant (Matthew 11:13; Luke 16:29).... The books of the Old Testament are thus called. We Christians, who have received the canon and rule of faith more enlarged, are said, 'to be built on the foundation of the prophets and apostles' (Ephesians 2:20); so that now the object of our faith is prophets and apostles." *Sermons on Acts 24:14–16*, 17:420.

the Scriptures, which impart to us "knowledge of those things which concern our faith, duty, and happiness."[10] Manton concludes, "Here we fix and rest, we have a sufficient rule, and a full record of all necessary Christian doctrine."[11]

Given his commitment to the sufficiency of Scripture, Manton rejects the Roman Catholics' contention that we are to receive "unwritten traditions" as Scripture. With equal conviction, he rejects the radicals' contention that we are to receive "new revelations" as Scripture.[12] He argues,

> When God sent his Son out of his bosom to reveal the whole doctrine of faith at once, and to declare his Father's will with full authority and power, he fixed and closed up the rule of faith. So it was not fit that after him there should come any extraordinary nuncios and ambassadors from heaven, or any other should be owned as infallible messengers, but such as he immediately sent abroad in the world to disciple the nations. Therefore all extraordinary ways ceased, and we are left to the ordinary rule stated by Christ.[13]

---

10. For faith, see John 20:30–31. For duty, see Titus 2:12. For happiness, see 2 Tim. 3:15. Manton, *Scripture Sufficient*, 5:494–95.

11. Manton, *Scripture Sufficient*, 5:495. For Manton, the sufficiency of Scripture is confirmed in Abraham's response to Dives's request to send someone from the dead to warn his brothers. Abraham refuses, stating that if they did not believe the law and the prophets, they will not believe even if someone visits them from the dead (Luke 16:30–31). Manton concludes the following: "The word of God hath clearly the pre-eminence, and is a far more accommodate instrument to work upon the hearts of men than any extraordinary dispensation whatsoever." *Sermons on Luke 16:30–31*, in Manton, *Works*, 17:354. Manton revisits this text and its implications in *Sermon on Romans 10:5–9*, in Manton, *Works*, 18:245–46.

12. "Let us learn that we do not receive the illumination of the Spirit of God to make us condemn the external word, and take pleasure only in secret inspirations, like many fanatics, who do not regard themselves spiritual, except they reject the Word of God, and substitute in its place their own wild speculations." Calvin, *Commentary on the Book of Psalms*, 4:413. "The enthusiast is not satisfied with the light of the word. The delusion of his own heart dreams of a light within—an immediate revelation of the Spirit, independent of the word." Bridges, *Psalm 119*, 338.

13. Manton, *Scripture Sufficient*, 5:495–96. See Heb. 1:1–2.

Manton believes that "extraordinary ways" served a very specific purpose in God's plan—namely, to confirm His truth.[14] The works performed by the apostles served to prove that "they were teachers sent from God."[15] Their mission was extraordinary in that they received their call immediately from Christ just as He received His call immediately from the Father (John 17:18; 20:21). Moreover, their gifts were extraordinary in that they were able to perform signs and wonders. In this capacity, the apostles produced Scripture, thereby consigning "a rule for the use of the church in all ages."[16] With the passing of the apostolic age, the need for these extraordinary works ended. Manton explains, "After the faith of Christ was sufficiently confirmed, miracles ceased; and it was fit they should cease, for God doth nothing unnecessarily."[17]

Because of his commitment to the sufficiency of Scripture, Manton is suspicious of those who seek to revive miracles; furthermore, he rebukes those who "dream of some days of the Spirit, wherein we shall have a greater light than is in the Scriptures."[18] Those who con-

---

14. Thomas Manton, *Sermons on 2 Thessalonians 2*, in Manton, *Works*, 3:71.

15. Manton, *Sermons on 2 Thessalonians 2*, 3:72.

16. Manton, *Exposition of Jude*, 5:322.

17. Manton, *Sermons on 2 Thessalonians 2*, 3:73. See Heb. 2:2–4. For Manton's discussion of the cessation of miracles in relation to anointing with oil for healing, see *Exposition of James*, 4:444–49.

18. Manton, *Exposition of Jude*, 5:111–12. For many today, the "divine encounter" is above reason, meaning the spiritual life is not about growing in the knowledge of God but removing all affirmations concerning God until we arrive at silence—the bare communion of the soul with God. The goal is to reach union with God—a point at which the Creator/creature distinction is no longer perceived. Key to this is the contemplation of the spiritual, celestial, beautiful, or divine. "Experimental mystical theology is a pure knowledge of God which the soul receives in the bright darkness of some high contemplation, together with so intimate an experience of love that it is utterly lost to itself and united and transformed in God." G. B. Scaramelli, *A Handbook of Mystical Theology*, trans. by D. H. S. Nicholson (1913; repr., Berwick, Maine: Ibis Press, 2005), 15–16. Mysticism is an approach to knowing God based on kinship between the soul and God. The soul returns to God in either a pantheistic (God is all) or panentheistic (God comes through all matter) way. It obscures the ontological distinction between infinite Creator and finite creature. Mysticism is not dependent on God revealing Himself but rather ascending to God through various techniques. This includes the use of silence and solitude to empty the consciousness in order to ascend to God. The result is euphoria or ecstasy. In both the East (Orthodox Church) and West (Roman Catholic Church), there

tend for such things are "perverted by mystical interpretations."[19] For Manton, Scripture alone is a safe and sufficient rule to follow because it is "the infallible revelation of God, delivered to the church by the prophets and apostles...and sealed by miracles and operations of the Holy Ghost, who was the author of them."[20] Since we possess a "perfect

---

is a strong emphasis on mysticism, stretching back to the early church. We seek communion with Him beyond written revelation, following the *scala perfectionis* (stages of perfection): the *purgative* life (asceticism); the *illuminative* life (learned ignorance); and the *unitive* life (union with God). This threefold path to God is paradigmatic for the mystical tradition in both the Roman Catholic and Orthodox traditions. Although the language of mysticism might *seem* biblical, it is important to note that all mystics stand in the same tradition. "This overcoming of all the usual barriers between the individual and the Absolute is the great mystic achievement. In mystic states we both become one with the Absolute and we become aware of our oneness. This is the everlasting and triumphant mystical tradition, hardly altered by differences of clime or creed. In Hinduism, in Neo-Platonism, in Sufism, in Christian mysticism, we find the same recurring note, so that there is about mystical utterances an eternal unanimity which ought to make a critic stop and think, and which bring it about that the mystical classics have, as has been said, neither birthday nor native land. Perpetually telling of the unity of man with God, their speech antedates languages, and they do not grow old." William James, *The Varieties of Religious Experience* (London: Collins, 1960).

19. Manton, *Exposition of Jude*, 5:232. Manton categorizes the Libertines, Quakers, Ranters, and Familists together, as those "looking for new discoveries." *Exposition of Jude*, 5:270. There are three types of mysticism. The first is epistemological: knowledge of God comes by way of internal intuition or illumination or revelation. The second is metaphysical: knowledge of God comes when our being is absorbed into the divine being. The third is ethical (or spiritual): knowledge of God is a result of our identification with Christ and filling with the Holy Spirit. Manton is a "mystic" in the third sense but certainly not the first two.

20. Thomas Manton, *Sermons on Romans 6*, in Manton, *Works*, 11:174. Manton warns, "How credulous we are to fables, and how incredulous as to undoubted truths; spirits and apparitions, these things are regarded by us, but the testimony of the Spirit of God speaking in the scriptures is little regarded." *Sermons on Luke 16:30–31*, 17:360–61. Again, "I might take occasion hence to press you to bless God for transmitting such a doctrine to us, and to give you caution not to look after other revelations; there are none, or, if there were, none can be so certain and sufficient as this. And whatever is pretended as a message from God, bring it to the scriptures (Isa. 8:20).... Some cry up the church; some the Spirit, in contradiction to the Scriptures. Do you take the middle course; go to the word opened and dispensed in the church, and wait for the Spirit's teaching; and whatever is pretended, if it be not according to this, there is no light in it; and if there be no light of knowledge, there will be no light of comfort, and no light of happiness." *Sermons on Luke 16:30–31*, 17:371.

canon," all we require is "ordinary revelation" whereby the Holy Spirit reveals God to us.[21]

When the Spirit accompanies the Word, it becomes the instrument of God's power in the lives of His people. In other words, the efficacy of God's Word lies in "the Spirit's assistance."[22] "The power is of God," says Manton, "yet it is wonderfully joined with the word; it is not enclosed in it, but sent out together with it when God pleaseth."[23] The Holy Spirit "joineth his power and efficacy with the proper instituted means—the word, which is the sword of the Spirit (Ephesians 6:17)."[24] God's Word, therefore, is the instrument by which God's Spirit produces "all his great effects in the souls of men."[25]

All of this means, in the words of the psalmist, that only the "entrance" of God's Word "giveth light" (Ps. 119:130).[26] For Manton, this penetrating light contains four "excellent properties," the focus of the next four chapters.

---

21. Manton, *Sermons on John 17*, 10:201. The only instance in which Manton acknowledges "immediate revelation" is assurance. But even this is "flitting and inconstant," leading to "new scruples and doubts." The better way is "the trial by grace." It is more "constant and durable." *Exposition of James*, 4:258.

22. Thomas Manton, *Exposition of Isaiah 53*, in Manton, *Works*, 3:210. See 1 Thess. 1:5.

23. Manton, *Sermons on John 17*, 10:228. See also *Exposition of James*, 4:116–17, 128–29, 151–52.

24. Manton, *Sermons on Romans 8*, 12:81. Elsewhere, Manton writes, "God concurreth with his own ordinance by his omnipotent and creating power." *Sermon on Acts 24:25*, in Manton, *Works*, 18:362.

25. Manton, *Sermons on Ephesians 5*, in Manton, *Works*, 19:411. In short, it is "the prescribed appointed means, without which we cannot look for any such things as a work of grace upon us." *Sermons on 1 Peter 1:23*, in Manton, *Works*, 21:333. For a detailed analysis of how the Spirit of God uses the Word of God in conversion, see *Sermons on Acts 2:37–38*, in Manton, *Works*, 21:237–98. For a detailed analysis of how the Spirit of God uses the Word in regeneration, see *Sermons on 1 Peter 1:23*, 21:298–336.

26. Manton, *Psalm 119*, 8:352–53.

Chapter 10

A Manifesting Light

To begin with, God's Word is a "manifesting" light.[1] The psalmist prays, "Open thou mine eyes, that I may behold wondrous things out of thy law" (Ps. 119:18).[2] Manton explains that when God answers this prayer, He does not grant "new revelations" but "a clear sight of what is already revealed."[3] God's truth is plainly revealed in Scripture, yet He must remove the "natural darkness and blindness that is upon our understandings."[4] He does so by infusing spiritual light. This work of illumination is not "simple nescience" (knowing the truth), "grammatical knowledge" (repeating the truth), or "dogmatical knowledge" (articulating the truth), but "experimental knowledge" (living the truth). It is, says Manton, "applicative," "affective," and "transformative."[5] He adds, "When the work of grace is expressed by knowledge, a theoretical and notional knowledge is not understood, but that which is practical and operative; such a knowledge as doth work such a change both in the inward and outward man, as that mind, heart, and practice do

---

1. *Lux manifestans.*

2. See also Ps. 119:105, 130. "The 'opening' is a divine activity. It results in the wonders that are in the Word being displayed in such a way that they have an immense and lasting effect on the one whose mind is informed and whose heart is inflamed." Jones, *Psalm 119 for Life*, 124.

3. Manton, *Psalm 119*, 6:164.

4. Manton, *Psalm 119*, 6:342.

5. Manton, *Psalm 119*, 6:166–67. For more on this, see *Sermons on Philippians 3*, in Manton, *Works*, 20:52–58. "External knowledge is like the child spelling the letters without any apprehension of the meaning." Bridges, *Psalm 119*, 39.

express a conformity to God's law."[6] Appealing to Psalm 119, Manton believes the impact of this manifesting light is evident in relation to three sociological contexts.

Wiser than Enemies

"Thou through thy commandments hast made me wiser than my enemies: for they are ever with me" (Ps. 119:98). According to the psalmist, God is the author of wisdom ("Thou"), while Scripture is the means by which He imparts wisdom ("through thy commandments").[7] Furthermore, he makes it clear that we become wise not through a "slight looking" into Scripture but through "an intimate constant acquaintance" with Scripture ("for they are ever with me").[8] The wisdom that Scripture imparts far exceeds that of the psalmist's enemies. How so?

Manton answers this question by explaining that wisdom consists of three things: choosing a "right end," adopting "apt and proper means" to achieve the chosen end, and pursuing the adopted means with "accurateness and diligence."[9] He proceeds to explain that the psalmist's enemies (and all unbelievers, for that matter) choose the world as their end, adopt the means to achieve their end, and pursue them with all their heart. This, in Manton's estimation, is *worldly wisdom*. In marked contrast, the psalmist chooses the enjoyment of God as his end, adopts God's Word as the rule by which he seeks to achieve his end, and consequently makes religion his main business—avoiding all evils and improving all occasions in order to "come to the enjoyment of the blessed God."[10] For Manton, this is *heavenly wisdom*.

---

6. Manton, *Psalm 119*, 7:271. Manton adds, "It is not a speculative light, or a bare notion of things.... It is such a learning as the effect will necessarily follow, such a light and illumination as doth convert the soul, and frame our hearts and ways according to the will of God." *Psalm 119*, 6:65. "When the wonderful character of God's testimonies is apprehended; and when their entrance has given light to the soul; something far beyond ordinary affection and desire is excited." Bridges, *Psalm 119*, 340.

7. Manton, *Psalm 119*, 7:485. See James 1:5, 17. For more on wisdom, see Thomas Manton, *Sermon on Proverbs 3:17*, in Manton, *Works*, 18:367–75.

8. Manton, *Psalm 119*, 7:487.

9. Manton, *Psalm 119*, 7:488.

10. Manton, *Psalm 119*, 7:488.

We possess this heavenly wisdom when, first, we prefer a higher good before a subordinate good.[11] We choose God as our portion because we know that whoever has God inherits "all things" (Rev. 21:7). Second, we possess heavenly wisdom when we prefer a profitable good before a pleasing good.[12] We see that the good of the soul is far more valuable than a little pleasure. Third, we possess heavenly wisdom when we prefer an eternal good over a temporal good.[13] Because we live forever, we need a happiness that lasts forever; thus, we look beyond temporal things to an eternal God as the source of our happiness. Finally, we possess heavenly wisdom when we prefer a necessary good over an arbitrary good.[14] We realize that riches, pleasures, and delights cannot contribute anything to our eternal happiness; rather, our happiness lies in the enjoyment of God. "He is the wisest man," declares Manton, "that takes God for his portion, and makes it his business to keep in with him."[15]

Wiser than Teachers

"I have more understanding than all my teachers: for thy testimonies are my meditation" (Ps. 119:99). The psalmist is claiming not to know more but to apply more than his teachers. For Manton, this captures the essence of true knowledge. It is not about how much we know; what matters is how much we apply. He remarks, "Practical knowledge is to be preferred before speculative, as much as the end is to be preferred before the means."[16]

Elsewhere, the psalmist prays, "Teach me good judgment and knowledge: for I have believed thy commandments" (Ps. 119:66). Manton carefully distinguishes between these two words: *knowledge* and *judgment*. The first is the "speculative perception" of truth, whereas the

---

11. Manton, *Psalm 119*, 7:488. See Matt. 6:33.
12. Manton, *Psalm 119*, 7:489. See Luke 12:15–21.
13. Manton, *Psalm 119*, 7:489.
14. Manton, *Psalm 119*, 7:489.
15. Manton, *Psalm 119*, 7:489.
16. Manton, *Psalm 119*, 8:10. Manton adds, "A mean Christian, that fears God, is a man of more understanding than he that hath a great deal of head-light."

second is the "practical application" of truth to life. This kind of judgment is of fundamental importance because it enables us to distinguish
between truth and error, good and evil, right and wrong;[17] determine
the right course of action in all conditions and circumstances;[18] and
direct our lives appropriately.[19]

Without sound judgment, we are prone to deception and weak in
the profession and practice of godliness. As a result, we "make religion
a burden to ourselves, or else a scorn to the world."[20] In sharp contrast, "The clearer our judgment is the more steadfast is our faith, the
more vehement our love, the more sound our joy, the more constant
our hope, the more calm our patience, the more earnest our pursuit of
true happiness."[21]

Wiser than Ancients

"I understand more than the ancients, because I keep thy precepts" (Ps.
119:100). According to Manton, the psalmist's point is that the understanding we obtain through God's Word is better than that which we
obtain through life's experiences (as represented by the ancients). Why?
Our experiences teach us a few things, but God's Word teaches us
everything related to true happiness. For the psalmist, this knowledge
is contingent on keeping God's precepts. There is, therefore, a direct
correlation between the practice of holiness and an "increase in spiritual understanding." Manton remarks, "Where there is a pure heart,
there is a great deal more clearness in the understanding. Reason and
fancy are dark, unless a man have a command over his passions and
affections; over his passions of anger, fear, grief; and over his affections
of love and joy, and appetite towards sensual delights."[22]

Our practice of holiness frees us to proclaim with the psalmist,
"How sweet are thy words unto my taste! yea, sweeter than honey to

---

17. Manton, *Psalm 119*, 7:203. See Heb. 5:14.
18. Manton, *Psalm 119*, 7:204.
19. Manton, *Psalm 119*, 7:205.
20. Manton, *Psalm 119*, 7:206–7.
21. Manton, *Psalm 119*, 7:208.
22. Manton, *Psalm 119*, 8:23. See 2 Peter 1:5.

my mouth!" (Ps. 119:103). In his sermon on this verse, Manton affirms that the soul has spiritual senses just as the body has physical senses.[23] There are three such senses mentioned in Scripture: *seeing* relates to faith;[24] *tasting* relates to "spiritual experience of the sweetness of God in Christ, and the benefits which flow from communion with him";[25] and *feeling* relates to the power of grace.[26]

This spiritual sense differs from a "bare and simple act" of the understanding. It is possible for us to know something that we do not feel, because there is a difference between apprehension and impression. "An apprehension of the sharpness of pain is not feeling of the sharpness of pain," says Manton. He adds, "We have notions of good and evil, when we neither taste the one nor the other. It is one thing to know sin to be the greatest evil, and another thing to feel it to be so; to know the excellency of Christ's love, and to taste the sweetness of it, this doth not only constitute a difference between a renewed man and carnal man, but sometimes between a renewed man and himself."[27] Unbelievers can talk about God's truth, but they never taste it. We, on the other hand, know something of its sweetness. We have a "real experience of the goodness of God in Christ," and this makes us love Him with all our hearts, choose Him as our portion, make His will our only rule, and "obey and serve him, whatever it cost."[28] This deep impression of God's excellencies on our hearts causes us "to relish and savor spiritual things."[29] This, in turn, enables us to discern between what is beneficial and hurtful to the soul. It also comforts us "in the sweetness of spiritual things" and preserves "the vitality of grace" within us.[30]

---

23. Manton, *Psalm 119*, 8:23. See 1 Peter 1:8.
24. See Heb. 11:27.
25. See Ps. 34:8.
26. See Phil. 3:10.
27. Manton, *Psalm 119*, 8:46.
28. Manton, *Psalm 119*, 8:46.
29. Manton, *Psalm 119*, 8:47.
30. Manton, *Psalm 119*, 8:47–48.

Conclusion

In sum, heavenly wisdom involves a constant acquaintance with God's Word ("for they are ever with me") (Ps. 119:98), a continual application of it ("for thy testimonies are my meditation") (Ps. 119:99), and consistent adherence to it ("because I keep thy precepts") (Ps. 119:100). We are wise when we govern our hearts and order our lives according to God's Word because we have set our hearts on the "right end"—the enjoyment of the blessed God.[31]

---

31. "These two—right affection and good understanding—are indispensably necessary to the due regulation of the life." Calvin, *Commentary on the Book of Psalms*, 4:450.

Chapter 11

A Directing Light

In addition to a manifesting light, God's Word is a "directing" light.[1] This is its second excellent property. "Thy word is a lamp unto my feet, and a light unto my path," declares the psalmist (Ps. 119:105). We are on a spiritual pilgrimage filled with perils and obstacles; thus, we require a guiding light. God has given us His Word to illumine our path, thereby showing us "the right way to our desired end."[2] "It is not," says Manton, "a light to our brains to fill us with empty notions, but a light to our feet to regulate our practice and to guide our actions."[3]

The Need for God's Direction

We are in desperate need of this light because we are incapable of finding the path and remaining on it without divine assistance. For this reason, the psalmist cries, "I am a stranger in the earth: hide not thy commandments from me" (Ps. 119:19). In his exposition of this verse, Manton makes it clear that we are "strangers" (or pilgrims) by way of "affection."[4] This means, first, that we are sensible of our frailty. We know we are but dust, and thus we pray, "Teach us to number our days,

---

1. *Lux dirigens.*

2. Manton, *Psalm 119*, 8:65. Manton adds, "There is a fourfold end wherefore God hath given us the Scriptures." (1) "That by this means heavenly doctrine might be kept free from corruption." (2) "That it might be read of all ages and of all sexes." (3) "For converting of men, or leaving them without excuse." (4) "That it might be a rule of faith and manners by which all doctrines are to be tried." *Psalm 119*, 8:71–72.

3. Manton, *Psalm 119*, 8:72.

4. Manton, *Psalm 119*, 6:174.

that we may apply our hearts unto wisdom" (Ps. 90:12). It also means
that we are dissatisfied with our present state. We know that this world
is not our home, and, therefore, we "groan within ourselves, waiting
for the adoption, to wit, the redemption of our body" (Rom. 8:23).
Finally, our status as pilgrims means that we have an interest in a better inheritance. We know we are sons of God and that "when he shall
appear, we shall be like him; for we shall see him as he is" (1 John 3:2).

For these reasons we count ourselves to be strangers on the earth.
This frame of mind is "proper to God's children" because we were "born
elsewhere."[5] Just as people love their native soil, we love our home and
consequently long for it. Since we are "partakers of the divine nature"
(2 Peter 1:4), we possess a strong inclination that disposes us to look
for another world. Our inheritance is there (Eph. 1:3). Our kindred are
there: God (Matt. 6:9), Christ (Col. 3:1), and the saints (Matt. 8:11).
Our abode is there. "An inn cannot be called our home," says Manton,
"where we come but for a night."[6]

Because he is a stranger, the psalmist pleads with God, "Hide not
thy commandments from me" (Ps. 119:19). Manton explains the connection between the psalmist's pilgrimage and plea as follows.[7] Our
status as strangers on this earth causes us to seek "a better and more
durable state." We cannot discover this better state on our own; therefore, we look to God, who has provided sufficient direction in His
Word. But we cannot understand God's Word apart from "the light of
the Spirit." For this reason, we ask God to give us His Spirit that we
might understand His Word.

---

5. Manton, *Psalm 119*, 6:174–75.

6. Manton, *Psalm 119*, 6:176. Manton explains what it means to behave as a
stranger: (1) "Avoid fleshly lusts. These cloud the eye, and besot the heart, and make
us altogether for a present good; they weaken our desires for heaven." (2) "Grasp not at
too much of the world; but what comes with a fair providence upon honest endeavors,
accept with thanks." (3) "If an estate comes in slowly, remember, a little will serve our
turns to heaven; more would be but a burden and snare." (4) "If God give abundance,
rest not in it with a carnal complacency." (5) "Keep up a warm respect to your everlasting home." (6) "Enjoy as much of heaven as you can in your pilgrimage, in ordinances,
in the first-fruits of the Spirit, in communion with saints." *Psalm 119*, 6:180–81.

7. Manton, *Psalm 119*, 6:181–82.

For Manton, our need for God's directing light is further heightened by our propensity to wander along the way. "I have gone astray like a lost sheep," declares the psalmist (Ps. 119:176). By virtue of our fallen condition, we stray naturally: "All we like sheep have gone astray" (Isa. 53:6). As sheep are prone to wander and become lost, we are prone to error because of our folly and obstinacy.[8] As sheep are incapable of finding their way back, we are incapable of setting ourselves on the right way. As sheep are inclined to follow blindly and unthinkingly, we are inclined to follow bad examples. "We easily swim with the stream," says Manton. As sheep are susceptible to danger once out of the fold or pasture, we are susceptible to "a thousand dangers."[9] We are, in short, "apt to turn out of the way that leadeth to God and true happiness."[10] This proneness continues even after conversion. "Though our heart was set to walk with God for the main," writes Manton, "yet we often swerve from our rule through ignorance or through inadvertency, and sometimes are blinded by worldly desires and fleshly lusts, and so transgress our bounds and neglect our duty."[11] For this reason, we stand in need of constant direction.

The Content of God's Direction

"Thy testimonies also are my delight and my counselors" (Ps. 119:24). What direction do we receive from God's Word?

In Our General Choice

To begin with, God's Word directs us to the remedy for "the miseries of the fall."[12] That is to say, it explains how we may be reconciled, converted, and come to the enjoyment of God.[13] Manton's understanding

---

8. Elsewhere, Manton distinguishes between those who err in the mind "out of frailty" and those who err in the heart "out of obstinacy." By nature, we do both and, therefore, "neglect," "oppose," and "despise" God. *Psalm 119*, 6:194–96.

9. Manton, *Psalm 119*, 9:301–3.

10. Manton, *Psalm 119*, 9:302.

11. Manton, *Psalm 119*, 9:303.

12. Manton, *Psalm 119*, 6:230. See Acts 20:27.

13. Manton, *Psalm 119*, 6:230. Manton states, "His mercy was from everlasting; for God, foreseeing the fall of Adam, provided us a remedy in Christ; and having all

of the gospel is rooted in his covenant theology. He believes that there are two covenants: a covenant of works and a covenant of grace. They agree in their author, meaning God established both—the covenant of works in Genesis 2:17 and the covenant of grace in Genesis 3:15.[14] They also agree in their "moving cause"—namely, God's grace. Although the second covenant is styled the covenant of grace, the first covenant was also of grace "though the condition of it was perfect obedience."[15] Additionally, the two covenants agree in their parties, in that God and man participate in both.[16]

According to Manton, the two covenants differ in their ends. The end of the covenant of works was "to preserve and continue man in that happiness...in which he was created." But the end of the covenant of grace is to restore "mankind to that happiness...from which he had fallen."[17] They also differ in their nature. The first covenant "stood more by commands, and less by promises," whereas the second covenant "stood more by promises, and less by commands."[18] Finally, they differ in their terms. "Unsinning obedience is the condition of the covenant of works," says Manton. It was made void by one sin, and it leaves us without "any hope of cure or remedy."[19] The covenant of grace, however, offers "pardon to sinners."

---

lapsed in his prospect and view, did out of his free love choose some, whilst others are passed by, to life and salvation by Christ. That God did from eternity decree and purpose this is manifest, because he doth in time effect it, otherwise he should not 'work all things according to the counsel of his will' (Eph. 1:11), or else his will would be mutable, willing that in time which he willed not from eternity." *Psalm 119*, 7:393.

14. Manton, *Psalm 119*, 8:371.

15. Manton, *Psalm 119*, 8:372.

16. Manton, *Psalm 119*, 8:372. Manton adds four additional points of commonality: (1) "God giveth sufficiency of strength...to the parties with whom he made them to fulfill the conditions thereof"; (2) "God kept up his sovereignty, and by his condescension did not part with anything of his dominion over man"; (3) "there is a mutual obligation on both parties"; and (4) "the conditions...were suitable to the ends and scope appointed." *Psalm 119*, 8:372–73.

17. Manton, *Psalm 119*, 8:374.

18. Manton, *Psalm 119*, 8:375.

19. Manton, *Psalm 119*, 8:376.

Manton teaches that, in the garden of Eden, God established the covenant of works with Adam and his posterity. That is to say, Adam stood in the place of his physical descendants, and God gave him a specific commandment. When Adam sinned, God counted his sin as his posterity's sin, his guilt as his posterity's guilt, and his punishment as his posterity's punishment. But Adam has a counterpart—the last Adam (Christ). For Manton, when we believe, we are no longer in Adam (under the covenant of works), because we have been united with Christ (under the covenant of grace), who has fulfilled the covenant of works on our behalf. This is the framework for Manton's understanding of "mutual imputation"—Christ fulfills the covenant of works, meeting its requirement by His active obedience (life) and paying its penalty by His passive obedience (death).

All who are under the covenant of grace are "made members of the mystical body of Christ."[20] From this union comes a communication of Christ and all His benefits unto us. Manton declares, "Christ first giveth himself to us, and with himself all things."[21] These benefits include three great blessings.[22] The first is justification, whereby God imputes righteousness to us. Because of this righteousness, "we are accepted with God."[23] The second is sanctification, whereby God imparts righteousness to us. He cleanses us from both the guilt and filth of sin.[24] The third is glorification, whereby God removes every last

---

20. Manton, *Psalm 119*, 9:106. For more on Manton's understanding of union with Christ, see *Sermons on John*, in Manton, *Works*, 11:23–31; and *Sermons on Romans 6*, 11:164–65, 182–83. For a full treatment of this subject in Puritan thought, see J. Stephen Yuille, *The Inner Sanctum of Puritan Piety: John Flavel's Doctrine of Mystical Union with Christ* (Grand Rapids: Reformation Heritage Books, 2007).

21. Manton, *Psalm 119*, 9:106.

22. Manton, *Psalm 119*, 6:60; 9:35.

23. Thomas Manton, *Life of Faith*, in Manton, *Works*, 15:56. See Rom. 1:17; Gal. 3:11. For Manton's handling of the doctrine of justification, see *Sermons on Hebrews 11*, in Manton, *Works*, 13:476–83.

24. As for the relationship between justification and sanctification, Manton states, "These two must not be severed; [they] must carefully be distinguished, but not separated." *Life of Faith*, 15:65. See 1 Cor. 1:30; 6:11. Of the two, sanctification is the greatest benefit. Why? (1) "Sin is worse than misery." Justification frees us from "pain and suffering," but sanctification frees us from "sin and pollution." (2) "The end must

vestige of sin from us. By the grace of justification "sin shall not damn"; by the grace of sanctification "sin shall not reign"; and by the grace of glorification "sin shall no longer be."[25] These benefits flow from our engrafting into Christ.

In Our Particular Actions

Second, God's Word directs us "in every particular action."[26] "Make me to go in the path of thy commandments; for therein do I delight" (Ps. 119:35). We need this directing Word so that we might "respect things according to their order and places, and give them precedency in our care and practice as their worth deserveth."[27] For example, we should serve and respect God before "our neighbors or ourselves";[28] prefer heaven before earth, and the salvation of our souls before the "interests and concernments" of our bodies;[29] choose present affliction rather than future;[30] give place to things that belong to godliness more than things of profit and pleasure;[31] and choose the greatest suffering "before the least sin."[32]

We also need this directing light so that we might walk in the way of holiness. "Wherewithal shall a young man cleanse his way?" asks the psalmist (Ps. 119:9).[33] His answer is by "taking heed" to God's Word.

---

be more noble than the means." Sanctification is the end of justification, as glorification is the end of sanctification. (3) "Ends are more noble, as they are nearest the last end." Justification is the pledge of the life of glory, but sanctification is the start of the life of glory. (4) "Real perfections are above relative." Sanctification is a real moral perfection, but justification is but a relative one; our state is changed by it, but not our hearts. *Life of Faith*, 15:67.

25. Manton, *Psalm 119*, 8:58.

26. Manton, *Psalm 119*, 6:231.

27. Manton, *Psalm 119*, 6:349.

28. See Acts 5:29.

29. See Matt. 6:33.

30. See 2 Cor. 5:18.

31. See 1 Tim. 6:6.

32. See Heb. 11:25. Manton, *Psalm 119*, 6:349–51.

33. "Never was there a more important question for any man." Charles Spurgeon, *The Golden Alphabet: A Devotional Commentary on Psalm 119* (Pasadena, Tex.: Pilgrim Publications, 1969), 41.

Commenting on this verse, Manton declares that the Bible serves, first, as the rule of holiness.[34] This means it reveals the only way of "reconciliation with God" (how to be cleansed from the guilt of sin) and the only way of "subjection to God" (how to be cleansed from the filth of sin).[35] The Bible serves, second, as the instrument of holiness; that is to say, God uses it to cleanse our hearts. "It is," says Manton, "the glass that discovers sin, and the water that washes it away."[36]

Conclusion

Our proneness to wander does not necessarily imply open declension from the way. It is usually far more subtle: spiritual disciplines are neglected, careless thoughts are indulged, and frivolous pursuits are entertained. If we are not actively seeking, we are wandering.[37] For this reason, we must actively seek God where He is found—namely, in His Word.[38] According to Manton, this seeking possesses three ingredients: "sincerity of aims," "integrity of parts," and "uniformity of endeavors."[39] It is summed up in the psalmist's cry: "I have refrained my feet from every evil way" (Ps. 119:101). Manton interprets *feet* as referring to the affections.[40] The condition of our affections (i.e., "the vigorous bent of the soul") determines our practice. If we love what is good and hate what is evil, our actions will follow accordingly.[41] When we devote ourselves to God's Word, it shapes our affections; in particular, it cultivates "a love to God" and "a fear of God."[42] These two graces, in turn, lead to

---

34. Manton, *Psalm 119*, 6:84.

35. For Manton's fullest treatment of the doctrine of sanctification, see *Sermons on Romans 6*, 11:153–379.

36. Manton, *Psalm 119*, 6:85. For more on this, see *Sermons on John 17*, 10:411–61; and *Sermons on Ephesians 5*, 19:477–86.

37. "Daily progress in the heavenly walk is not maintained by yesterday's grace." Bridges, *Psalm 119*, 21.

38. "He is therefore to be sought by means of it, or in accord with it, and certainly not apart from it or in contradiction to it." Jones, *Psalm 119 for Life*, 37.

39. Manton, *Psalm 119*, 6:92–94.

40. Manton, *Psalm 119*, 8:25.

41. Manton, *Psalm 119*, 8:28.

42. Manton, *Psalm 119*, 8:34–35. See Pss. 97:10; 119:13; Prov. 8:13; 13:12.

two duties: "watchfulness and resistance."[43] And these lead us to refrain "from every evil way."[44] For Manton, there is no erring while we walk by this directing light.[45]

---

43. Manton, *Psalm 119*, 8:35.
44. Manton, *Psalm 119*, 8:29–31.
45. Manton, *Psalm 119*, 8:41.

Chapter 12

A Quickening Light

In addition to a manifesting and directing light, God's Word is a "quickening" light. It possesses this excellent property because it is the means by which the Holy Spirit implants, maintains, and renews spiritual life within us.[1] The psalmist proclaims, "I will never forget thy precepts: for with them thou hast quickened me" (Ps. 119:93).[2]

Regeneration

To begin with, God quickens us by way of regeneration.[3] Manton describes this as "the first infusion of the life of grace."[4] Because of this infusion, we love what we formally hated (God), and we hate what we formerly loved (sin); that is to say, we turn "from the creature to God," "from self to Christ," and "from sin to holiness."[5] For Manton, this work of regeneration involves the three principal faculties of the soul: understanding, affections, and will. These faculties, characterized by knowledge, righteousness, and holiness, constitute the image of God in humanity (Eph. 4:24; Col. 3:10).[6] When Adam sinned, this

---

1. *Lux vivificans.*

2. See also Ps. 119:25, 37, 40, 50, 107, 149, 154, 156.

3. Manton, *Psalm 119*, 6:389–96, 435–38; 7:429–39; 8:102–4; 9:84–89. Elsewhere, Manton refers to regeneration as the "general enlargement" of the heart. Our heart is enlarged when we "are freed from the bonds of natural slavery, and the curse of the law, and the power of sin, to serve God cheerfully." *Psalm 119*, 6:325.

4. Manton, *Psalm 119*, 8:103. See also 6:395, 435.

5. Manton, *Psalm 119*, 7:439.

6. Manton, *Exposition of James*, 4:295–96.

image was corrupted. This does not mean that Adam lost his faculties (understanding, affections, and will) but that he lost knowledge, righteousness, and holiness. This deprivation had a negative impact on Adam's faculties in that his will was no longer directed by an understanding that knew God or by affections that desired God.[7] Instead, his understanding was darkened, his affections were hardened, and his will was enslaved.[8] And this has been the predicament of his posterity ever since.

Regeneration is the restoration of God's image, meaning the faculties of the soul are renewed in knowledge, righteousness, and holiness. God quickens His people by illuminating their darkened understanding, softening their hardened affections, and liberating their enslaved will. As a result of this renewal, we possess a new spiritual sense, and we take God as our "chief good" and "utmost end." God brings about this quickening through His Word: "Of his own will begat he us with the word of truth, that we should be a kind of firstfruits of his creatures"

---

7. According to the Augustinian principle, the natural gifts (understanding, affections, and will) remain in humanity but the supernatural gifts (knowledge, righteousness, and holiness) are gone. Lewis Bayly explains, "The felicity lost was, first, the fruition of the image of God, whereby the soul was like God in knowledge, enabling it perfectly to understand the revealed will of God; secondly, true holiness, by which it was free from all profane error; thirdly, righteousness, whereby it was able to incline all its natural powers, and to frame uprightly all its actions, proceeding from those powers." *The Practice of Piety: Directing a Christian How to Walk, That He May Please God* (1613; repr., Grand Rapids: Reformation Heritage Books, 2019), 32. Even earlier, William Perkins writes, "We must know that there were in Adam, before his fall, three things not to be severed one from the other; the substance of his body and soul; the faculties and powers of his body and soul; and the image of God, consisting in a straightness and conformity of all the affections and powers of man to God's will. Now, when Adam falls and sins against God, what is his sin? Not the want of the two former (for they both remained), but the very want and absence of the third thing, namely, of conformity to God's will." *The Whole Treatise of the Cases of Conscience, Distinguished into Three Books* (London, 1632), 6. When Adam was separated from God at the time of the fall, he was inclined to disobedience because this deprivation had a negative impact on his faculties. His will was no longer directed by an understanding that knew God or affections that desired God. This means that sin has no formal existence. According to Perkins, sin "is properly a want or absence of goodness." Perkins, *Cases of Conscience*, 7.

8. Manton adheres to Augustine's concept of the "bound" free will. In short, "our impotency lies in our obstinacy." *Exposition of Jude*, 5:481.

(James 1:18). According to what James says here, the efficient cause of regeneration is God's "own will," meaning it excludes compulsion on God's part and merit on our part. The instrumental cause of regeneration is "the word of truth." It is by means of the Word of God that the Spirit illumines our minds, thereby softening our hearts and liberating our wills so that we receive Christ through faith. The final cause of regeneration is "that we should be a kind of firstfruits of his creatures." In the Old Testament, the firstfruits of the harvest were set apart to God. Similarly, God quickened us to set us apart to Himself.[9]

While Manton stresses God's sovereignty in His quickening of sinners, he is also committed to explaining how we experience this new birth.[10] He identifies two main steps. The first is conviction: "The commandment, the law of God, breaks in with all its terrors and curses upon the soul by strong conviction, and the man is given for gone, lost, and dead."[11] When we see ourselves in the light of God's law, we perceive our sin. As a result, we recognize that we are without moral virtues adequate to commend ourselves to God. We acknowledge our utter dependence on God's grace. "None are converted," says Manton, but those who are "first convinced of their danger and evil estate."[12] Why? The language of faith is meaningless to those who remain unconvinced of their need for a savior.

The second step is compunction. According to Manton, we will not come to Christ, "the spiritual physician," unless we are "heart-sick." We must feel the "load upon [our] back" before we will seek for ease.[13] When we are convinced we suffer from a disease, we immediately call for the doctor. When the doctor arrives, we yield ourselves to his counsel and willingly accept whatever remedy he prescribes. The same is true when it comes to faith in Christ. When we are absolutely convinced of our need, we submit to God's cure. We grasp that we are beyond all

---

9. Manton, *Exposition of James*, 4:116–27.

10. For Manton on the doctrine of election, see *Sermons on 2 Thessalonians 2,* 3:102–12; *Exposition of James*, 4:90–91; and *Exposition of Jude*, 5:18, 39, 128–35.

11. Manton, *Psalm 119*, 7:439. See also *Exposition of Jude*, 5:21–24.

12. Manton, *Psalm 119*, 7:439.

13. Manton, *Psalm 119*, 7:440. See also *Sermons on Romans 8*, 12:103.

hope of attaining salvation on the basis of our righteousness. We realize
we deserve God's wrath. This is a despair that arises not from any doubt
concerning God's mercy but from our own inability. In other words,
we despair of saving ourselves. When we are deeply affected like this,
we become conscious of our sin, mindful of our need, and aware of our
need for a savior. Exhausted, we look beyond ourselves for assistance.
Having learned the disease of our spiritual inability and impotency, we
turn to Christ and desire Him and His merits. We hunger and thirst
after a righteousness that is not our own—"the righteousness of God
without the law" (Rom. 3:21).

Renewal

Because of God's quickening work (i.e., regeneration), we possess three
"advantages":[14] an *inclination* toward what is good,[15] a *preparation* of our
hearts for holy actions,[16] and a *power* to do good works.[17] The problem,
however, is that these "infused principles" weaken without God's ongo-
ing assistance.[18] "There may be life where there is no vigor," declares
Manton.[19] For this reason, we need a continual quickening whereby
God lifts us out of a "cold, sad, and heavy" condition and makes us
more lively.[20] In this work of renewal, God gives us His "quickening,

---

14. Manton, *Psalm 119*, 6:362–63.

15. See Rom. 6:13; Gal. 2:19.

16. See Eph. 2:10; 2 Tim. 2:21.

17. See Gal. 5:25; Col. 2:6.

18. For Manton's treatment of the causes and remedies for "decay" in godliness, see
England's Spiritual Languishings, in Manton, *Works*, 5:415–40.

19. Manton, *Psalm 119*, 6:239. Manton declares, "God's children are under deadness sometimes." *Psalm 119*, 7:429. Why? He points to unconfessed sin (Ps. 51:11),
neglect of spiritual duties (Phil. 2:12–13), ingratitude for God's benefits (Col. 2:7),
spiritual pride (James 4:6), and familiarity with the world (Ps. 119:37). *Psalm 119*,
7:429–37. See also Thomas Manton, *Sermons on 2 Thessalonians 3:5*, in Manton, *Works*,
2:242–45, 253–55.

20. Manton, *Psalm 119*, 7:429. See also 6:395. Elsewhere, Manton describes this
work of renewal as a "particular enlargement" of the heart—"the actual assistance of the
Lord's grace, carrying us on in the duties of our heavenly calling with more success."
Psalm 119, 6:327.

actuating, assisting grace" to improve the three infused principles so that their operations are "carried forth with more success."[21] Manton describes this quickening as God breathing "upon his own work."[22] When the fire is about to go out, we add fuel to the embers. Soon, the fire is ablaze. Similarly, when our spiritual life wanes in intensity, we ask God to quicken us. And He does so by His Word.

We often lie "under deadness of heart" and, therefore, we must pray to God, asking Him, "who is the fountain of grace, to emit and send forth his influences."[23] This is the psalmist's experience: "My soul cleaveth unto the dust: quicken thou me according to thy word" (Ps. 119:25).[24] Here the psalmist describes himself as a man mortally wounded in battle, lying prostrate on the ground, gasping his final breath.[25] Again, he cries, "My soul melteth for heaviness: strengthen thou me according unto thy word" (Ps. 119:28). He is overcome with grief and unable to find relief anywhere. This spiritual condition stems from outward pressures and inward griefs.[26] According to Manton, this condition is the result of our unstable heart, which never remains in the same condition: "Now it is up, and anon it is down."[27] Our flesh opposes us because it sets "desires against desires, and delights against

---

21. Manton, *Psalm 119*, 6:363. Manton remarks, "Many Christians look for rapt and ecstatic motions.... Sense, appetite, and activity are the fruits of life and quickening." *Psalm 119*, 9:85.

22. Manton, *Psalm 119*, 8:103.

23. Manton, *Psalm 119*, 6:240. For Manton, the "feeling of spiritual deadness" is not a bad thing per se, because it proves that "some life and sense" still remain. Only those who know God's quickening work in regeneration are able to "bemoan" themselves to God. *Psalm 119*, 9:84.

24. Spurgeon says the psalmist "sought that blessing which is the root of the rest." *Golden Alphabet*, 73. Again, "We ought greatly to admire the spiritual prudence of the psalmist, who does not so much pray for freedom from trial as for renewed life that he may be supported under it. When the inner life is vigorous, all is well" (182).

25. Manton, *Psalm 119*, 6:235.

26. Manton, *Psalm 119*, 6:236. God permits these seasons of spiritual decline to correct us for past sins, humble us in the midst of our "great enjoyments," try our graces to see if we will depend on Him in difficult times, awaken us to pray, and show His glory—namely, the "riches of his goodness" in our recovery. *Psalm 119*, 6:236.

27. Manton, *Psalm 119*, 9:86–87.

delights."[28] Our "outward condition" perplexes us because worldly troubles discourage us while worldly comforts exalt us—both bringing "deadness upon the heart."[29] Finally, our "careless walking" unsettles us because it dampens "the quickening influences of [God's] Spirit."[30] For all these reasons, we require God's quickening work: "the renewing and increasing in vigor of spiritual life."[31] Such vigor enables us "to move and act towards God as [our] utmost end, to glorify him, or to enjoy him."[32]

Quickening in Duty

God must provide this quickening grace amid duty. When it comes to spiritual duties such as praying, meditating, worshiping, and reading God's Word, we are prone to "weariness and uncomfortableness," which causes us to "hang off from God."[33] As a result, a "deadness of spirit" soon creeps on us.[34] This condition is our own fault. It arises from our negligence or slothfulness;[35] we still struggle with a "strong bias of corruption" that draws us away from Christ to present things.[36] It also arises from our "carnal liberty";[37] we expend so much time and effort on the vanities of the world and the pleasures of the flesh that deadness engulfs our hearts.[38] In times like these, we need God to quicken us by exciting the "operative graces"—faith and love.[39] "These are the graces wherein life consists," says Manton, "and as these are acted and excited

---

28. Manton, *Psalm 119*, 9:87. The flesh is "drawing" (James 1:14), "depressing" (Heb. 12:1), and "warring" (Rom. 7:23).

29. Manton, *Psalm 119*, 9:88.

30. Manton, *Psalm 119*, 9:88.

31. Manton, *Psalm 119*, 9:84. "More life means more love, more grace, more faith, more courage, more strength." Spurgeon, *Golden Alphabet*, 272.

32. Manton, *Psalm 119*, 8:196.

33. Manton, *Psalm 119*, 6:272. For more on this, see Thomas Manton, *How May We Cure Distractions in Holy Duties*, in Manton, *Works*, 5:443–57.

34. Manton, *Psalm 119*, 8:103.

35. Manton, *Psalm 119*, 8:103. See also 6:395–96; and 2 Tim. 1:6.

36. Manton, *Psalm 119*, 6:240. See Heb. 12:1.

37. Manton, *Psalm 119*, 8:103. See Ps. 119:37.

38. Manton, *Psalm 119*, 8:103.

39. Manton, *Psalm 119*, 8:103. Manton is quick to note that we must also seek to

to God, so we are lively."[40] God quickens our faith by giving us a sense of His power, and He quickens our love by giving us a sense of His goodness.[41] The result is spiritual strength to perform spiritual duties.[42]

Quickening in Affliction

God must also provide this quickening grace amid affliction.[43] At times, "vehement sorrow" overwhelms us, and we languish under a deep sense of present trouble.[44] God responds to our cries by "reviving our suffering graces," such as faith, hope, and patience, thereby enabling us to "go on cheerfully in our service."[45] He revives these graces by impressing on us the sense of His love (Rom. 5:5) and the hope of glory (Rom. 5:2–3).[46] This "shining of God's face... is the reviving of afflicted spirits," declares Manton.[47] As we turn to God's Word, we "apprehend and apply God's love to the soul."[48] We behold His particular providence, His fatherly care, the example of Christ, the promise of the Holy Spirit,

---

"stir up ourselves." We must perform duties even in the "case of deadness and indisposition." *Psalm 119*, 6:240–42.

40. Manton, *Psalm 119*, 6:240.

41. Manton, *Psalm 119*, 6:436.

42. Manton states, "We are sluggish, and loath to stir a foot in the ways of obedience, therefore God must enlarge. From first to last God does all in the work of grace; he giveth the habit and act; he planteth graces in the heart, knowledge, faith, love, and delight; and then he exciteth and quickeneth them to act." *Psalm 119*, 6:332.

43. "In deep affliction, the greatest want is the want of more spirituality—more liveliness in the cause of God. Blessed is he who so interprets providence as thereby to be led to a closer walk with God." Plumer, *Psalms*, 1067. "This is the best remedy for tribulation; the soul is raised above the thought of present distress, and is filled with that holy joy which attends all vigorous spiritual life, and so the affliction grows light." Spurgeon, *Golden Alphabet*, 207.

44. Manton, *Psalm 119*, 6:265. See also 6:395; 8:104.

45. Manton, *Psalm 119*, 6:240.

46. For more on hope and comfort amid affliction, see Thomas Manton, *Sermon on Job 19:25*, 2:293–306; *Sermon on Hebrews 12:1*, 2:411–23; *Sermon on 1 Corinthians 7:30*, 2:425–37; *Sermon on 1 Corinthians 15:57*, 2:441–54; *Sermon on Revelation 14:13*, 2:457–75; *Sermons on 2 Corinthians 5*, 12:423–94, 13:303–15; *Sermons on Titus 2:11–14*, 16:172–218; *Sermons on Romans 4:18–21*, 17:179–89; and *Sermons on 2 Corinthians 4:18*, 18:274–94.

47. Manton, *Psalm 119*, 6:239.

48. Manton, *Psalm 119*, 8:197.

and the hope of glory. God impresses these truths on the heart, thereby reviving us "in all our languishings."[49] The result is spiritual strength to endure affliction.

"LORD, I have hoped for thy salvation, and done thy commandments" (Ps. 119:166). Whereas faith holds the candle to our soul so that we see "things invisible and to come," hope makes the light "comfortable and ravishing to us."[50] In short, it is "the expectation of some future good."[51] Hope is necessary "to quicken and enliven our duties." When we hope for something, we will become "engaged in the thorough pursuit of it."[52] Hope is necessary to "sharpen our affections after heavenly things." It does so by stirring up "serious thoughts" of the blessedness to come and "hearty groans" after it. These set both the mind and heart to work.[53] Hope is necessary to put the heart at rest, allaying "our disquiets, and fears, and cares, and sorrows, that so we may go on cheerfully in God's service." It functions like an anchor in the midst of the storm, keeping our mind in "a constant temper in the midst of the stormy gusts of temptation." It quiets our hearts by assuring us that "things will end well at last, how blustering and stormy soever the weather be at present."[54]

Conclusion

For Manton, God delights to work by means.[55] This is certainly the case when it comes to His quickening work: "God will not bless any other doctrine so much as the Word to quicken, revive, and comfort the soul; and therefore here we should busy ourselves, for it contains the surest grounds of comfort, and the Spirit is associated with it, and

---

49. Manton, *Psalm 119*, 7:432.

50. Manton, *Psalm 119*, 9:220.

51. Manton, *Psalm 119*, 9:219.

52. Manton, *Psalm 119*, 9:221.

53. Manton, *Psalm 119*, 9:221.

54. Manton, *Psalm 119*, 9:222.

55. Manton, *Psalm 119*, 7:433. Manton declares, "There is the Spirit acting, and the habit of grace acted upon, and the word and sacraments are the instruments and means." *Psalm 119*, 9:85.

goes along with it, to bless it to our souls."[56] For Manton, God's Word is the means by which God produces within us "serious and ponderous thoughts," which work directly on our affections.[57] He stirs up thoughts of His "high and glorious" authority to awe us, His "wonderful love in Christ" to constrain us, the "reasonableness" of His commands to invite us, the "joys" of heaven to allure us, and the "horrors of everlasting darkness" to keep us in "a lively sense of our duty."[58] God reveals these great truths in His Word, thus making it a quickening light.

---

56. Manton, *Psalm 119*, 7:433. For Manton, the Holy Spirit works in "concomitancy" with the Word. See Isa. 30:20; 49:21. He adds, "The Spirit of God rides most triumphantly in his own chariot."

57. Manton, *Psalm 119*, 7:432.

58. Manton, *Psalm 119*, 7:432.

Chapter 13

A Comforting Light

Thus far we have seen that God's Word is a manifesting, directing, and quickening light. Manton adds one more excellent property to this list: God's Word is a "comforting" light.[1] The psalmist declares, "Let, I pray thee, thy merciful kindness be for my comfort, according to thy word unto thy servant" (Ps. 119:76).[2] God's "merciful kindness" is His willingness to do good to those who are miserable.[3] Our misery arises from our difficult circumstances—our troubles weigh heavy on us, thereby weakening our submission to and confidence in God.[4] But in the midst of our "doubts, fears, and sorrows,"[5] God communicates His merciful kindness to us through His Word.[6] By this means, our "faith is confirmed," our "love is increased," and our "hope is enlivened."[7] For Manton, this is "the business and design of Scripture." It brings us "to believe in God, and to wait upon him for our salvation."[8]

---

1. *Lux exhilarans.*

2. See also Ps. 119:26, 50, 52.

3. Manton, *Psalm 119*, 7:301.

4. Manton, *Psalm 119*, 7:153–54. For Manton's thoughts on why we should expect troubles in this world, see his sermons on Luke 9:57–62: *The Faithful Followers of Christ Must Expect Troubles in This World*, in Manton, *Works*, 2:113–39.

5. Manton, *Psalm 119*, 7:305.

6. Manton, *Psalm 119*, 8:353. See also 6:221–24, 271–73; 7:29–38, 301–4, 331–35, 423–27; 9:23–24.

7. Manton, *Psalm 119*, 7:47.

8. Manton, *Psalm 119*, 7:28.

The Danger of Fainting

"My soul fainteth for thy salvation: but I hope in thy word. Mine eyes fail for thy word, saying, When wilt thou comfort me? For I am become like a bottle in the smoke; yet I do not forget thy statutes" (Ps. 119:81–83). Here the psalmist states that his soul is fainting;[9] that is to say, his "spiritual strength" is abating.[10] This is the result of "the tediousness of [his] present sorrows and pressures."[11] His predicament is so desperate that he says he has "become like a bottle in the smoke." The picture here is of a wineskin heated over a fire until it becomes dried out and begins to crack. As this wineskin is "dry and wrinkled and shrunk up," so too the psalmist is "worn out and dried up with sorrow and long suspense of expectation."[12] For this reason, he implores God: "When wilt thou comfort me?" In his cry he acknowledges that it is God's comfort alone that can keep him from fainting.[13]

Opposition

The psalmist's prayer is particularly relevant in times of opposition: "Remove from me reproach and contempt; for I have kept thy testimonies. Princes also did sit and speak against me: but thy servant did meditate in thy statutes" (Ps. 119:22–23).[14] Reproach will come to those who stand for the truth. The best way to ease the heart in such times is to meditate on God's merciful kindness as revealed in His Word. Manton declares, "There is matter enough to take up our thoughts and allay our cares and fears, and to swallow up our sorrows and griefs, to direct us in all straits."[15] God's Word teaches us to look away from man to God: "There is a higher judge that sits in heaven."[16]

---

9. Manton differentiates between two kinds of fainting: that which causes "dejection and trouble" and that which causes "defection and falling off from God." *Psalm 119*, 7:355. See also *Sermons on Romans 8*, 12:227–28.

10. Manton, *Psalm 119*, 7:354.

11. Manton, *Psalm 119*, 7:355.

12. Manton, *Psalm 119*, 7:373.

13. Manton, *Psalm 119*, 7:305.

14. See also Ps. 119:42.

15. Manton, *Psalm 119*, 6:221.

16. See also Heb. 11:27.

It also teaches us to look away from providence to the covenant: "Providence is a very riddle; we shall not know what to make of it till we gather principles of faith from the covenant."[17] And it teaches us to look away from temporal things to eternal things: "A feather or a straw against a talent, a man would be ashamed to compare them together."[18]

When we look away from man to God, from providence to the covenant, and from temporal things to eternal things, we grow in trust: "an exercise of faith, whereby, looking upon God in Christ through the promises, we depend upon him for whatsoever we stand in need of, and so are encouraged to go on cheerfully in the ways wherein he hath appointed us to walk."[19] When we trust God, we are committing ourselves to His power and referring ourselves to His will.[20] This removes our fears, allays our sorrows, and banishes our cares.[21]

Desertion

The psalmist's prayer is also relevant in times of desertion: "How many are the days of thy servant?" (Ps. 119:84). The urgency behind the question is heightened by God's apparent inactivity and hostility. "Though we fly to God's help, yet sometimes God may withdraw and forsake us," explains Manton.[22] On such occasions, we sense that God is absent from our prayers. Moreover, we perceive that we lack His lively influence.[23] Thus, we cry, "Let thy tender mercies come unto me, that I may

---

17. See also Heb. 13:5.

18. See also 2 Cor. 4:17–18.

19. Manton, *Psalm 119*, 6:449.

20. Manton, *Psalm 119*, 6:451. See also 7:54–55.

21. Manton, *Psalm 119*, 6:453.

22. Manton, *Psalm 119*, 6:77. See also 8:409–11. Manton identifies two sins for which God often "deserts" the soul: carnal liberty and spiritual laziness.

23. According to Manton, God allows such times to correct us for our sins, acquaint us with weaknesses, subdue our self-confidence, increase our esteem of Christ, value the suffering of Christ (i.e., "the bitter cup of which he drank for us"), and prevent greater evil to come by subduing our pride. *Psalm 119*, 6:80; 7:21–22. Manton provides the following directions to help us to navigate seasons of desertion. (1) "Observe God's comings and goings." (2) "Inquire after the reason." (3) "Submit to the dispensation." (4) "Learn to trust in a withdrawing God, and depend upon him." (5) "Pray." (6) "Give thanks that God is not wholly gone." *Psalm 119*, 6:81–82.

live" (Ps. 119:77). Without a "sense of God's favor and good-will," we feel like dead men; but when God reveals His merciful kindness to us, it is like "a resurrection from the dead."[24]

There is nothing more precious to the believer than God's favor: "Make thy face to shine upon thy servant; and teach me thy statutes" (Ps. 119:135). When the sun shines its light and spreads its heat, the creatures are "cheered and revived." Conversely, when the sun is obscured, the creatures "droop and languish." For Manton, "What the sun is to the outward world, that is God to the saints."[25] In times of desertion, we turn to God's Word. It reminds us of His love in Christ, and a sense of divine love "is the sweetest thing that ever we felt, and is able to sweeten the bitterest cup that ever believer drank of."[26]

The Remedy for Fainting

"Unless thy law had been my delights, I should then have perished in mine affliction" (Ps. 119:92). Evidently, the psalmist views God's Word as the remedy for fainting. Why? It points us to God, "the true fountain of all comfort."[27] It points us to Christ, "the meritorious and procuring cause" of all comfort.[28] It also points us to the Holy Spirit, "the applier of all comfort."[29] In addition to directing our focus heavenward, God's Word is the actual instrument by which God comforts us. According to Manton, it makes provision for our comfort. How so?

First, it comforts by way of its commands.[30] God's Word commands us to deny ourselves: "If any man will come after me, let him deny himself, and take up his cross, and follow me" (Matt. 16:24). If we were to love the world less, we would be troubled less when our interest in the world suffers loss. "The greatness of our affections causeth

24. Manton, *Psalm 119*, 7:310.
25. Manton, *Psalm 119*, 8:408. See Num. 6:25; Ps. 67:1.
26. Manton, *Psalm 119*, 8:413.
27. Manton, *Psalm 119*, 7:423. See 2 Cor. 1:3.
28. Manton, *Psalm 119*, 7:423. See 2 Thess. 2:16.
29. Manton, *Psalm 119*, 7:423. See Rom. 15:3.
30. Manton, *Psalm 119*, 7:31. See also 9:23.

the greatness of our afflictions," says Manton.[31] Moreover, God's Word charges us "to moderate our sorrow, to cast all our care upon God, to look above temporal things, and hath expressly forbidden distracting cares, and doubts, and inordinate sorrows."[32]

Second, God's Word comforts us by way of its doctrines.[33] "Thou art my hiding place and my shield: I hope in thy word," declares the psalmist (Ps. 119:114). "God is a hiding-place to keep us out of danger, and a shield to keep us in danger."[34] His Word declares it (Gen. 17:1) and assures us of divine protection (Ps. 18:30).[35] Manton focuses on God's "particular" providence, celebrating the fact that God looks after each of His own as if He had no one else to care for.[36] "This is a mighty ground of comfort," declares Manton. God has taken us into His family, and all His doings are "paternal and fatherly."[37] His fatherly care flows from His unchangeable love for His people: "When our outward condition doth vary and alter, we have the same blessed God as a rock to stand upon, and to derive our comforts from, that we had before."[38] Out of His love for us, He uses our troubles to humble, mortify, and correct us, so that we might be "more capable of heavenly glory."[39]

Third, God's Word comforts us by way of its examples.[40] It points us to the farmer who plants his seed, then "waiteth for the precious fruit of the earth" (James 5:7). It also points us to the prophets who spoke "in the name of the Lord" and endured the people's hated because of it (James 5:10). God's Word also points us to Job, who fixed his eyes on God amid crushing circumstances (James 5:11). As a result of God's dealings with him, Job learned that God is "very pitiful and of tender

---

31. Manton, *Psalm 119*, 7:32.
32. See Matt. 10:26–28; Phil. 4:6; 1 Peter 5:7.
33. Manton, *Psalm 119*, 7:32.
34. Manton, *Psalm 119*, 8:168.
35. Manton, *Psalm 119*, 8:171.
36. Manton, *Psalm 119*, 7:32. See also 7:50–51, 414–15.
37. Manton, *Psalm 119*, 7:33. See Matt. 6:32; Heb. 12:5–7.
38. Manton, *Psalm 119*, 7:33. See also Rom. 8:36.
39. Manton, *Psalm 119*, 7:33.
40. Manton, *Psalm 119*, 7:34.

mercy." God had compassion for his afflictions and mercy for his sins. All of these serve as examples to us. Manton remarks, "God doth not call us by any rougher way to heaven than others have gone before us."[41]

Fourth, God's Word comforts us by way of its promises.[42] It promises us that God has pardoned our sins (Rom. 5:1). There is no "true cure for sorrow" until we are exempt from God's wrath. It also promises us that we possess eternal life (Rom. 5:2). Eternal joy counterbalances "all that we can endure and suffer." Furthermore, it promises us that God meets our temporal needs (Rom. 8:28). God disposes all things "for the best to them that love him."[43] Through the promises, God's Word draws our mind away from "things present to things future," and demonstrates the "excellency and certainty of these future things."[44] The Holy Spirit applies these comforts by God's Word (Rom. 15:13), and we receive them through faith (Heb. 11:1).[45]

Fifth, God's Word comforts us by way of its principles.[46] Manton enumerates various examples. God knows our needs, and He is able to relieve them.[47] Those who wait on God's providence will receive "present support" or "final deliverance."[48] God frustrates the "designs of

---

41. Manton, *Psalm 119*, 7:34.

42. Manton, *Psalm 119*, 7:34. See also 9:23.

43. See Manton, *Sermons on Romans 8*, 12:59–75.

44. Manton, *Psalm 119*, 7:358.

45. Manton explains how we should "carry ourselves" toward the promises in *Works*, 9:284. (1) "You must rest confident of the truth of what God hath promised, and be assured that in time the performance will come to pass, as if you saw it with your eyes." See Heb. 10:22; 11:13. (2) "You are to delight in the promise, though the performance be not yet, nor like to be for a good while." See Heb. 11:13. (3) "You are to take the naked promise for a ground of your hope, however it seem to be contradicted in the course of his providence. It is his word you are to go by, and stand by, and according to which you must interpret all dispensations." See Rom. 4:18. (4) "This faith must conquer our fears, and cares, and troubles.... The force of faith is seen in calming our passions and sinful fears; or else it is but a notion, and our reverence and respect to God will be weakened by it." See Ps. 112:7. (5) "When faith hath done its work in the quieting of our own hearts, you must glorify God in your carriage before others." See 1 Thess. 1:5–7.

46. Manton, *Psalm 119*, 7:331–33.

47. See Matt. 6:32.

48. See Isa. 40:31.

wicked men."[49] The proud will fall.[50] God never abandons us amid difficulties.[51] He usually works by "contraries" because "the gospel way to save is to lose."[52] God brings honor through shame, happiness through misery, comfort through sorrow, and life through death. By all these principles, God teaches us "to hope against hope."[53]

Conclusion

For these reasons, God's Word alone is the remedy for fainting. The psalmist proclaims, "Concerning thy testimonies, I have known of old that thou hast founded them for ever" (Ps. 119:152). According to Manton, the testimonies of God stand on two foundations: "the unchangeableness of God's nature (Hebrews 6:18)" and "the blood of Christ (1 Corinthians 3:11)."[54] This is a great source of comfort to God's people.[55] It reminds us that although "our estate and condition is many times changed," God's Word "is no more changed than himself is changed."[56] It also reminds us that in times of confusion "there is a God in heaven, who will judge not according to the opinions of the times, but according to the reality of things revealed in his holy word."[57]

God's Word is, therefore, a strong comfort. All other comforts are weak because they are susceptible to affliction, death, and judgment. In addition, it is a full comfort, speaking to every conceivable trouble: "No strait can be so great, no pressure so grievous, but we have full consolation offered us in the promises against them all." Finally, it is a reviving comfort in that "faith penetrates into the inwards of a man,

---

49. See Ps. 37:12–13.

50. See Prov. 16:5.

51. See Heb. 13:5.

52. See Matt. 16:25.

53. See Rom. 4:18.

54. Manton, *Psalm 119*, 9:115.

55. Manton writes, "To depend upon an invisible God for a happiness that lieth in an invisible world, when in the meantime he permitteth us to be harassed with difficulties and troubles, requireth faith." *The Excellency of Saving Faith*, in Manton, *Works*, 2:140. This brief work (2:140–61) consists of two sermons on Heb. 10:39 and 1 Peter 1:9.

56. Manton, *Psalm 119*, 9:117.

57. Manton, *Psalm 119*, 9:117.

does us good to the heart; and the soul revives by waiting upon God, and gets life and strength."[58] God's Word assures us of God's "favorable acceptance": "Great peace have they which love thy law: and nothing shall offend them" (Ps. 119:165).[59] We enjoy the peace that comes from having God as our friend, and we are comforted with "a true sense and apprehension of his love and favor."[60]

---

58. Manton, *Psalm 119*, 7:29.

59. "Here is the happiness of a child of God summed up in one word—peace." Bridges, *Psalm 119*, 435.

60. Manton, *Psalm 119*, 9:208.

Chapter 14

Spiritual Duties

As the psalmist declares, it is the "entrance" of God's Word alone that "giveth light" (Ps. 119:130). As the Holy Spirit illumines our mind and inclines our heart, the Bible becomes a manifesting, directing, quickening, and comforting light. As such, it is, for Manton, the means through which God imparts His blessedness to us. This means that the Spirit of God speaks to us through the Word of God, making its histories, promises, warnings, truths, prophecies, and doctrines come alive to us, thereby enlarging our faith. According to Manton, faith is "a grace by which we believe God's word."[1] He affirms that it is the root of all other graces: "Love works, hope waits, patience endures, zeal quickens to own God's truth and cause, obedience urges to duty; but faith, remembering us of our obligations to Christ and presenting the hopes of a better life, has the greatest stroke in all these things."[2] In addition, Manton believes that faith produces effects such as spiritual sense, taste, feeling, strength, and affection; in short, it causes us to "relish spiritual things."[3] These are the returns we make to God as He impresses His Word on our hearts.

For Manton, this is the essence of spiritual life—moving to God "as our last and utmost end," serving Him "as our greatest scope," and

---

1. Manton, *Life of Faith*, 15:48. See also Thomas Manton, *Sermons on 2 Thessalonians 1:3*, in Manton, *Works*, 17:110.

2. Manton, *Life of Faith*, 15:50.

3. Manton, *Life of Faith*, 15:53.

enjoying Him "as our chief good."[4] Again, the great instrument by which this spiritual life is produced is faith,[5] and the great instrument by which faith is "fed and increased" is God's Word.[6] The whole Word of God is the object of our faith: its histories are for our warning, its doctrines for our admiration, its threatenings for our humiliation, its precepts for our subjection, and its promises for our consolation.[7] Thus, the whole Word of God has its use: its histories "make us wary and cautious," its doctrines "enlighten us with a true sense of God's nature and will," its precepts "regulate our obedience," its promises "cheer and comfort us," and its threatenings "terrify us."[8]

For Manton, the conclusion is obvious: "Without the word there can be no faith."[9] Spiritual life, therefore, depends on hearing and reading God's Word.[10] It is the means by which God sends His life-giving

---

4. Manton, *Life of Faith*, 15:47.

5. Manton, *Life of Faith*, 15:48.

6. Based on Rom. 10:14–15, Manton affirms that God's Word is the means "to beget and breed" faith. *Sermons on 2 Thessalonians 1:3*, 17:126. It is "the seed of new life" (1 Peter 1:23; James 1:18). It is "the constant rule of all our actions" (Ps. 119:105, 110, 133). It is "the charter of our hopes" (John 20:31; 1 John 5:11). It is "our strength and preservative against all temptations from the devil, the world, and the flesh" (Eph. 6:17; 1 John 2:14). It is "our comfort and cordial in our afflictions" (Ps. 119:59, 92; Heb. 12:5). *Sermons on 2 Thessalonians 1:3*, 17:131–33.

7. Manton, *Life of Faith*, 15:158.

8. Manton, *Life of Faith*, 15:158.

9. Manton, *Life of Faith*, 15:163. If faith comes by hearing the Word, then how can faith be necessary to make the Word effectual? Manton explains, "At first God by his preventing grace taketh hold of the heart, and maketh it to believe; as at the first creation light was made before the sun; and the first man was made out of the dust of the ground, afterwards he propagateth and bringeth forth after his kind; so that the first work might be exempted from the common rule, yet not the subsequent works." *Life of Faith*, 15:170.

10. See Deut. 32:45–47; John 6:68; 1 Cor. 2:11–13; Gal. 3:2. "Human beings cannot get properly oriented in life without digesting words…. The Spirit in authentic Christian spirituality is the Spirit who speaks in the Scriptures…. He continues to accompany those writings whenever they are studied and preached." Mark Talbot, "Growing in the Grace and Knowledge of Our Lord and Savior Jesus Christ," in *For All the Saints: Evangelical Theology and Christian Spirituality*, ed. Timothy George and Alister McGrath (Louisville, Ky.: Westminster John Knox, 2003), 130, 133.

Spirit.[11] As the Spirit of God works through the Word of God, the latter becomes a manifesting, directing, quickening, and comforting light whereby we commune with the living God.[12] Our realization of this leads us to a zealous pursuit of God's Word. In short, we "busy ourselves" with it.[13] This is the reason why Manton places such importance on the practice of spiritual duties (the means of grace),[14] such as reading, hearing, meditating, praying, singing, using the seals, and keeping the Sabbath.[15] These are the instruments through which the Spirit of God produces faith in the people of God.[16] We must, therefore, "be

11. See John 3:1–8; 1 Peter 1:22–25.

12. "We are sustained in the journey of faith by the means of grace.... Chief among the means of grace is the Bible, understood not only as a deposit of divine revelation but also as the meeting place of the believer and the living Christ; the sacraments (some evangelicals prefer the term *ordinances*) of baptism and the Lord's Supper, understood not as 'mere' symbols devoid of real spiritual power but rather as the enacted Word of God that effectually conveys the promise and presence of Christ by faith; the life of prayer, both private and communal; and the act of preaching, through which the living voice of the gospel is conveyed to the gathered congregation." Timothy George, introduction to *For All the Saints*, 5.

13. Manton, *Psalm 119*, 7:433.

14. Manton, *Life of Faith*, 15:55. See Thomas Manton, *Sermons on Matthew 25*, in Manton, *Works*, 9:345–46, 396; and *Sermons on John 17*, 10:144–45; 11:12–14. Lewis Bayly maintains that the essence of piety is "to join together, in watching, fasting, praying, reading the Scriptures, keeping his Sabbaths, hearing sermons, receiving the holy Communion, relieving the poor, exercising in all humility the works of piety to God, and walking conscionably in the duties of our calling towards men." *Practice of Piety*, 163. According to E. Glenn Hinson, this statement sums up "the whole Puritan platform." "Puritan Spirituality" in *Protestant Spiritual Traditions*, ed. F. C. Senn (New York: Paulist Press, 1986), 165.

15. Manton, *Sermons on Titus 2:11–14*, 16:155–60.

16. There are conflicting views on the means of grace. (1) Roman Catholicism collapses any distinction between sign and reality. In other words, the sign is the reality. The seven sacraments of the church—baptism, Communion, confession, penance, marriage, ordination, and extreme unction—are the means by which God's grace is conveyed to individuals regardless of their spiritual condition. These sacraments are efficacious (successful) in and of themselves, for all who participate in them. By participating, people perform the works necessary to be saved by God's grace. (2) Popular evangelicalism separates sign and reality. Sacraments are merely human acts. The ordinances of baptism and Communion are strictly human activities. (3) Historic confessionalism recognizes the relationship between sign and reality without collapsing the two. The issue is not divine presence but divine action. The Father gave the Son to us, objectively, in history.

diligent in the use of the means of grace," whereby we receive "further measures and degrees" of the Holy Spirit.[17]

The psalmist states, "And I will delight myself in thy commandments, which I have loved. My hands also will I lift up unto thy commandments, which I have loved; and I will meditate in thy statutes" (Ps. 119:47–48). Here the psalmist expresses his resolve to employ all his faculties with God's Word.[18] With his mind he will meditate on God's Word, and he will delight in it with his affections. As a result of his meditating and delighting, he will "lift up" his hands to obey God's Word. For Manton, the relationship between these three—knowing, loving, and obeying—is pivotal.

Now the Father gives the Son to us, objectively, in the Word and sacraments. Yet we must receive Him. Therefore, the sacraments are not efficacious in and of themselves for all who participate in them. They are the appointed vehicles through which God chooses to work in the lives of His people.

17. Manton, *Sermon on 1 John 2:20*, in Manton, *Works*, 22:103.

18. Manton, *Psalm 119*, 7:12.

Chapter 15

Meditating

"I will meditate in thy precepts, and have respect unto thy ways" (Ps. 119:15).[1] When it comes to the spiritual duties, Manton believes that meditation is of supreme importance because it enlivens all the others: "Meditation is the life of all the means of grace, and that which makes them fruitful to our souls."[2] Related to this, he believes that meditation is "the great fuel of faith."[3] That is to say, it is the means by which faith is begotten and increased.[4]

When he speaks of meditation, Manton does not mean the act of reading, whereby we gather information from Scripture, or the act of hearing, whereby we listen to sermons based on Scripture.[5] He argues that, apart from meditation, reading and hearing are like "a winter

---

1. For the psalmist's meditation on God's Word, see Ps. 119:23, 27, 48, 78, 97, 99, 148. Manton is so convinced of the importance of meditation that he warns his readers, "The beast under the law that did not chew the cud was unclean." *Exposition of James*, 4:160.

2. Manton, *Psalm 119*, 7:479. Manton rebukes those who minimize the importance of meditation: "Young and green heads look upon meditation as a dull melancholy work, fit only for the phlegm and decay of old age; vigorous and eager spirits are more for action than thoughts, and their work lieth so much with other that they have no time to descent into themselves." *Sermons on Genesis 24:63*, in Manton, *Works*, 17:264. "No spiritual exercise is more profitable to the soul than that of devout meditation." Spurgeon, *Golden Alphabet*, 54.

3. Manton, *Sermons on Hebrews 11*, 13:376.

4. Manton, *Sermons on Hebrews 11*, 13:377.

5. Manton, *Psalm 119*, 6:105–6.

sun that shineth, but warmeth not."[6] It is only by seriously pondering God's Word that it enters into the "very heart."[7]

The Need for Meditation

According to Manton, there is a "power of the soul" that lies between our senses and understanding, which makes our thoughts real and vivid. This power captures the affections, which, in turn, direct the will.[8] When the soul's faculties are rightly governed, practice follows affection, which follows persuasion, which follows knowledge. Because of the fall, however, this order is subverted: "Objects strike upon the senses, sense moveth the fancy, fancy moveth the bodily spirits, the bodily spirits move the affections, and these blind the mind and lead the will captive."[9] In our fallen condition, our senses have become the "*cinque ports* by which sin is let out and taken in."[10] When they hold sway, we lose sight of God's greatness, righteousness, and loving-kindness, the majesty of Christ, the beauty of grace, and the reality of eternity. These truths become mere abstractions and, as a result, our affections lose order, our mind loses focus, and our will chooses sin.

"I hate vain thoughts: but thy law do I love," declares the psalmist (Ps. 119:113). According to Manton, these vain thoughts consist of "carnal discourses," "carnal musings," and "carnal devises."[11] We are

---

6. Manton, *Psalm 119*, 6:140. Manton adds, "Reading and hearing are effectual by meditation." *Psalm 119*, 9:80. Again, "The heart is hard and the memory slippery, the thoughts loose and vain; and therefore, unless we cover the good seed, the fowls of the air will catch it away." *Psalm 119*, 6:141.

7. Manton, *Psalm 119*, 6:106. Manton adds, "We taste things better when they are chewed than when they are swallowed whole." *Psalm 119*, 9:80.

8. Manton, *Psalm 119*, 6:351.

9. Manton, *Psalm 119*, 6:351.

10. Manton, *Psalm 119*, 6:389–90.

11. Manton, *Psalm 119*, 8:157–58. Manton unpacks the nature of vain thoughts. He speaks of their "slipperiness and inconstancy." They wander here and there, especially "when we are employed in holy things." He also speaks of their "unprofitableness and folly." Because they are fixed on "frivolous things," they are of no benefit to us or others. Finally, he speaks of their "carnality and fleshliness." They are stirred by carnal desire or carnal delight—a longing for worldly things. *Psalm 119*, 8:158–59.

"pestered" with these thoughts.[12] "The mind of man is always working," warns Manton, "and if it be not fed and supplied with good matter, it works upon that which is evil and vain."[13]

The Practice of Meditation

We must, therefore, devote ourselves to meditation whereby "we come to be more thoroughly acquainted with the mind of God revealed in his word."[14] Water is naturally cold, but fire makes it hot, causing it to boil. Likewise, our hearts are naturally cold, but meditation makes them hot, causing them to boil with love for God and His Word. "If you mean to keep in the fire, you must ply the bellows and blow hard," counsels Manton.[15] Scripture meditation is the vehicle by which what is known in the head seeps down into the heart. Without it, we muse on trifles and that which is evil—uncleanness, revenge, envy, pride, and covetousness.[16] By it, we reflect the light of truth into our souls. As we meditate on God's Word, the Holy Spirit illumines our spiritual eyes (Eph. 1:18).

There is "occasional" meditation by which "the soul spiritualizes every object about which it is conversant."[17] Manton is chiefly con-

---

12. Manton, *Psalm 119*, 8:164.

13. Manton, *Psalm 119*, 8:165. Manton adds, "He that hath more silver and gold in his pocket than brass farthings, brings forth gold and silver oftener than brass."

14. Manton, *Psalm 119*, 7:19. See Prov. 2:4; Rom. 12:2. Manton's practice of meditation stands in marked contrast to the mystical tradition. See appendix 2. "Contemplation was a unifying principle in Origen's cosmos:... Behind this was the Platonic idea of the soul's kinship with the divine: it was this kinship that made contemplation possible and which was realized in contemplation.... Neither for Plato nor for Origen were souls created: they were pre-existent and immortal. The most fundamental ontological distinction in such a world was between the spiritual and the material. The soul belonged to the former realm in contrast to its body which was material: the soul belonged to the divine, spiritual realm and was only trapped in the material realm by its association with the body." Andrew Louth, *The Origins of the Christian Mystical Tradition from Plato to Denys* (Oxford: Clarendon Press, 1981), 76–77. For exemplars of this tradition, see Brother Lawrence, *The Practice of the Presence of God*; Teresa of Avila, *Interior Castle*; and Thomas Merton, *The Seven Storey Mountain*.

15. Manton, *Psalm 119*, 7:80.

16. Manton, *Psalm 119*, 6:144–45. See also 8:160–61.

17. Manton, *Psalm 119*, 6:139. See also 7:79.

cerned, however, with "set and solemn" meditation,[18] which he defines
as "that duty and exercise of religion whereby the mind is applied to
the serious and solemn consideration and improvement of the truths
which we understand and believe, for practical uses and purposes."[19]
Again, this is not a mere reading or studying of Scripture but a *purpose-ful* reading and studying of Scripture. When we meditate on God's
Word, we digest it; that is, we bring its truths to remembrance so that
we might consider them until they are impressed "upon the heart."[20]
Simply put, its goal is the internalization of God's Word. It is a dwelling or reflecting on Scripture, a musing or mulling over the biblical
text, whereby the truths of God's Word grips the three main faculties
of the soul.[21]

---

18. Manton, *Psalm 119*, 6:140. See also 7:79. Manton identifies three sorts of
meditation. (1) "There is a meditation of observation, when a man compares the word
and providence, and is still taking notice how such a promise is accomplished, such
a threatening made good" (see Ps. 107:43). (2) "There is the meditation of study and
search, they that are inquiring into the word of God to find out his mind" (see Eph.
5:17). (3) "There is a meditation of consideration, when we consider that which we read
and hear, how it may be for use and practice, and of what moment it is for our eternal
weal or woe" (see 2 Tim. 2:7). *Psalm 119*, 8:12–13.

19. Manton, *Psalm 119*, 6:140. Manton identifies three kinds of "solemn and set"
meditation. The first is *reflexive*: "a solemn parlay between a man and his own heart
(Psalm 4:4)." We function as our own accuser and judge as we examine our lives in the
light of Scripture. The second is *dogmatical*: "when we exercise ourselves in the doctrines
of the word, and consider how truths known may be useful to us." The third is *practical*:
"when we take ourselves aside from worldly distractions, that we may solemnly debate
and study how to carry on the holy life with better success and advantage." *Sermons on
Genesis 24:63*, 17:268–69.

20. Manton, *Psalm 119*, 6:138. "It is the digestive faculty of the soul, which converts the word into real and proper nourishment: so that this revolving of a single verse
in our minds is often better than the mere reading of whole chapters." Bridges, *Psalm
119*, 31. For more on Puritan meditation, see J. Stephen Yuille, "Conversing with God's
Word: Scripture Meditation in the Piety of George Swinnock," *Journal of Spiritual Formation and Soul Care* 5 (2012): 35–55.

21. A faculty-focused approach to meditation is widespread among the Puritans.
J. I. Packer observes, "Knowing themselves to be creatures of thought, affection, and
will, and knowing that God's way to the human heart (the will) is via the human head
(the mind), the Puritans practiced meditation, discursive and systematic, on the whole
range of biblical truth.... In meditation the Puritan would seek to search and challenge
his heart, stir his affections to hate sin and love righteousness, and encourage himself

First, we ponder God's Word in the mind.[22] As we do the hard work of study, we apply our minds to sacred subjects as they appear in God's Word.[23] Second, we impress the truth of God's Word on the affections.

with God's promises." *Quest for Godliness*, 24. Horton Davies defines the goal of Puritan meditation as "moving from intellectual issues to exciting the heart's affections in order to free the will for conformity to God." *Worship and Theology in England from Andrewes to Baxter and Fox, 1603–1690* (Princeton, N.J.: Princeton University Press, 1975), 119. In a similar vein, Peter Toon states, "In meditation a channel is somehow opened between the mind, heart, and will—what the mind receives enters the heart and goes into action via the will." *From Mind to Heart: Christian Meditation Today* (Grand Rapids: Baker, 1987), 18. In terms of the affections specifically, he states, "Meditation was seen as a divinely appointed way of stimulating or raising the affections toward the glory of God." *From Mind to Heart*, 94.

22. For Manton, the mind is the supreme faculty of the soul. This does not mean the will necessarily follows the dictates of the mind but rather that the knowledge of God always begins in the mind because the will cannot choose what the mind does not know. In affirming the temporal priority of the mind, William Perkins remarked, "The mind must approve and give assent, before the will can choose or will: and when the mind has not power to conceive or give assent, there the will has no power to will." *A Reformed Catholic; or, A Declaration Showing How Near We May Come to the Present Church of Rome in Sundry Points of Religion, and Wherein We Must Forever Depart from Them*, in *Works of William Perkins* (London, 1608), 1:553. The Enlightenment was determined to overthrow any "supernatural" view of reality. For this reason, it rejected any concept of revelation, and it championed human reason as the sole authority. Ultimately, this led to skepticism. Immanuel Kant responded to the skepticism of David Hume by constructing a theory of knowledge that excluded the possibility of knowing God with the mind. Today, many evangelicals have divorced faith from reason, accepted the "unreasonableness" of the faith, and adopted a suspicious view of the mind. Paul's emphasis on the mind stands in marked contrast to the prevailing trend. He does not speak of the Holy Spirit directly touching our soul. He does not contrast the work of the Holy Spirit and the exercise of the mind. He does not conceive of spirituality without the mind (Rom. 12:2). On the contrary, for Paul, the Holy Spirit works through the mind to edify and sanctify us. We are not to pursue a religious experience but rather to grow in our knowledge of the truth. We should seek to be rational. By rational, we mean in accord with reason. "If our minds are dull and lifeless, then our Christian lives will reflect it. If our minds are filled with great thoughts about Christ, which then filter into our affections, our lives will show that He stands at their center." Ferguson, *From the Mouth of God*, 159.

23. Manton says that we must begin with "pregnant thoughts." This means we set our "hearts to consider the subject, for when the heart is once set, these thoughts through the blessing of God will come in freely." *Sermons on Genesis 24:63*, 17:303. From here, we proceed to "serious enforcements." These include the following: by *arguments* we

Manton affirms that "our affections follow our apprehensions" because there is no way to come to the heart but by the mind.[24] If we remove the pot of water from the fire before it boils, it will quickly cool. Similarly, if we leave off meditation before the affections are fully engaged, our enthusiasm will quickly wane. Manton explains that we possess "two great influencing affections—love and hatred."[25] The first serves for "choice and pursuit," while the second serves for "flight and aversation." The great work of meditation is to fix these two on "their proper objects." He warns, "Our faith, our love, our desires, our delight, they are all acted and exercised by our thoughts; so that the spiritual life is but an imagination, unless we do frequently and often take time for serious meditation of him."[26]

Third, we express the truth of God's Word with the will. When love is set on God, and hatred is set on sin, the motions of the soul function properly. As a result, we take God as our happiness, His Son as our Savior, His Spirit as our guide, His Word as our rule, His holiness as our desire, and His promises as our hope. In this way, meditation is "the mother and nurse of knowledge and godliness."[27]

The Focus of Meditation

"Make me to understand the way of thy precepts; so shall I talk of thy wondrous works" (Ps. 119:27). For Manton, God's Word displays His "wondrous works," thereby furnishing us with numerous subjects worthy of meditation. Specifically, we meditate on "God, that we may love him and fear him"; "sin, that we may abhor it"; "hell, that we may avoid it"; and "heaven, that we may pursue it."[28] Manton exhorts,

---

consider "causes and effects." The first increases our knowledge, while the second stirs our affections. By *similitudes* we come to understand "spiritual things" through our consideration of "sensible things." By *comparisons* we put "contraries" together so that they might serve to "illustrate one another." By *colloquies* and *soliloquies* we ask questions of ourselves. *Sermons on Genesis 24:63*, 17:304.

24. Manton, *Psalm 119*, 8:61–62.
25. Manton, *Psalm 119*, 8:155.
26. Manton, *Psalm 119*, 7:80.
27. Manton, *Psalm 119*, 9:80.
28. Manton, *Psalm 119*, 6:144.

"Meditate upon the doctrines, promises, threatenings, man's misery, deliverance by Christ, necessity of regeneration, then of a holy life, the day of judgment. Fill the mind with such kind of thoughts, and continually dwell on them."[29]

One of the most profitable subjects for meditation is God Himself.[30] "I have remembered thy name, O LORD, in the night, and have kept thy law" (Ps. 119:55).[31] In his sermon on this verse, Manton notes the psalmist's practice: "I have remembered thy name, O LORD." The psalmist is "addicted to God," meaning he has taken "God for his happiness, his word for his rule, his Spirit for his guide, and his promises for his encouragement." As a result, his heart is always "working towards God day and night,"[32] meaning he remembers God's name. Manton affirms that there is a twofold remembrance.[33] The first is "notional and speculative" when we recall things with the mind; it consists of "barren notions" and "sapless opinions." The second is "practical and affective" when we recall things with the heart; it consists of "lively and powerful impressions," which produce "reverence, love, and obedience."[34] In short, "we remember God so as to love him, and fear him, and trust in him, and make him our delight, and cleave to him, and obey him."[35]

Meditation on God stirs three "radical" graces:[36] thoughts of His power produce fear, thoughts of His wisdom produce faith, and

---

29. Manton, *Psalm 119*, 7:481. Elsewhere, Manton mentions the following subjects as worthy of meditation: the great end of man, the evil of sin, the misery of the world, the vanity of the creature, the horror of death, the severity of judgment, the torment of hell, the excellencies of Christ, the privileges of the gospel, the mystery of providence, and the glory of heaven. *Sermons on Genesis 24:63*, 17:303.

30. Christ also figures prominently in Manton's meditation. By way of example, see *Exposition of Isaiah 53*, 3:187–494.

31. For the psalmist's remembrance of God's Word, see Ps. 119:22, 30, 44, 51, 55, 56, 59, 60, 61, 67, 69, 83, 87, 88, 93, 94, 100, 101, 102, 104, 109, 110, 115, 117, 129, 141, 153, 157, 161, 166, 168, 173, 176.

32. Manton, *Psalm 119*, 7:76.

33. Manton, *Psalm 119*, 7:77–78.

34. Manton, *Psalm 119*, 7:78.

35. Manton, *Psalm 119*, 7:77.

36. Manton comments, "This is the blessed employment of the saints, that they may live in the consideration and admiration of this wonderful love." *Psalm 119*, 7:89.

thoughts of His goodness produce love.[37] We should keep our thoughts on God until "we admire him" and "we make some practical improvement of him."[38] A "sight of God" will draw us away from the creature by causing us to abase "all things beside God, not only in opinion but affection."[39] It will draw us away from self by revealing our "vileness and misery" in the light of God's glorious majesty.[40] It will draw us away from sin by showing us that it is "a deformity to God."[41] Finally, a sight of God will draw us to Him in faith, love, and fear.[42] This, in turn, will comfort us in adversity and restrain us in prosperity.

"For ever, O LORD, thy word is settled in heaven. Thy faithfulness is unto all generations: thou hast established the earth, and it abideth. They continue this day according to thine ordinances: for all are thy servants" (Ps. 119:89–91). In one of his sermons on these verses, Manton dwells on God's eternality. He muses on the fact that God is infinite, "without beginning or ending."[43] In viewing God, we are "enclosed between infiniteness before and infiniteness behind." Whichever way we look, we see "infiniteness round about."[44]

Manton bemoans the fact that God's eternality "is not seriously and sufficiently enough thought of and improved, till it lessen all other things in our opinion and estimation of them and affection to them."[45] There is nothing that promotes "the great ends of the gospel" as much as meditation on God's eternality.[46] First, it makes Christ precious. He is the only one who can deliver us from the wrath to come and procure for us the eternal enjoyment of God: "No good thing will he withhold from them that walk uprightly" (Ps. 84:11). Second, it promotes

---

37. Manton, *Sermons on 2 Corinthians 5*, 13:148.

38. Manton, *Psalm 119*, 7:92.

39. Manton, *Psalm 119*, 7:92.

40. Manton, *Psalm 119*, 7:93.

41. Manton, *Psalm 119*, 7:93.

42. Manton, *Psalm 119*, 7:93.

43. Manton, *Psalm 119*, 7:391.

44. Manton, *Psalm 119*, 7:392.

45. Manton, *Psalm 119*, 7:396. Manton adds, "The whole drift of our religion is to call us off from time to eternity, from this world to a better." *Psalm 119*, 7:398.

46. Manton, *Psalm 119*, 7:399.

change. It makes "a proud man humble, a vain man serious, a covetous man heavenly, [and] a wicked man good." Third, it checks temptations. It demonstrates that the pleasures, riches, and honors of this world are but "transitory things." Fourth, it quickens diligence, showing us what is truly important: "Wherefore do ye spend money for that which is not bread? and your labor for that which satisfieth not?" (Isa. 55:2).

The Fruit of Meditation

In Manton's opinion, meditation is "not a thing of arbitrary concernment…but of absolute use, without which all graces wither."[47] It is of such importance because it fastens truths on "the mind and memory," shows the beauty of divine truths, prevents vain thoughts, and nurtures knowledge and godliness.[48] "Those that do often and seriously keep God in their thoughts," says Manton, "will be most careful to keep his commandments."[49]

"I will meditate in thy precepts, and have respect unto thy ways" (Ps. 119:15). Manton believes the relationship between the two clauses in this verse is extremely significant. In short, meditation "will beget a respect to the ways of God."[50] The psalmist declared, "Thy word have I hid in mine heart, that I might not sin against thee" (Ps. 119:11). In

---

47. Manton, *Psalm 119*, 6:141. The subject of meditation appears repeatedly throughout Manton's collected works. His most extensive treatment is found in *Sermons on Genesis 24:63*, 17:263–350. For Manton's rules for meditation, see appendix 1.

48. Manton, *Psalm 119*, 6:143. See also 7:19, 479–82; 8:12–13.

49. Manton, *Psalm 119*, 7:80. "This habit of love and holy meditation will spread its influence over our whole character. It will fill our hearts with heavenly matter for prayer, diffuse a sweet savor over our earthly employments, sanctify the common bounties of providence (1 Timothy 4:4–5), realize the presence of God throughout the day, command prosperity upon our lawful undertakings (Psalm 1:3), and enlarge our usefulness to the church (1 Timothy 4:15)." Bridges, *Psalm 119*, 248.

50. Manton, *Psalm 119*, 6:138. See Josh. 1:8; Phil. 4:8–9. The relationship between meditation and obedience, and the consequent blessing, is developed in Ps. 1. The blessed man meditates on God's law "day and night" (Ps. 1:2). The verb *meditate* is a frequentative imperfect; hence, it is a continuous act. Thus the righteous man is characterized by a daily routine of meditation on God's Word. Interestingly, the conjunction *and* in verse 3 is part of a strong *waw* consecutive verb. This indicates the presence of a result clause. In other words, the individual who meditates on God's Word is blessed. How? There is a fourfold description in verse 3. He is blessed because he is like a tree

his sermon on this verse, Manton notes, first, the psalmist's *practice*: "Thy word have I hid in mine heart." We store up things in one of two ways—either to conceal them or to cherish them. Manton believes the latter is in view in this verse: "What we value most preciously we save most carefully."[51] We store God's Word in our hearts through knowledge of it, assent to it, and "serious and sound digestion of it."[52] That is to say, we do not study God's Word in a cursory manner, for a mere acquaintance with God's Word will not do us any good.[53] Instead, we "ponder it seriously, that it may enter into [our] very heart."[54]

Manton notes, secondly, the psalmist's *purpose*: "that I might not sin against thee."[55] How does "storing up the Word" inhibit sin? It prevents vain thoughts because "the mind works upon what it finds in itself." Further, it furnishes us with material so that we can counsel, comfort, and reprove others. It supplies us in prayer because it makes God's promises real and enlarges our affections so that we are better able to pour out our hearts before Him. Storing up God's Word helps us in all businesses and affairs by urging us to duty, restraining us from sin, directing us in our ways, and seasoning our work. It guards us

---

planted by rivers of water, he brings forth fruit in season, his leaf does not wither, and whatever he does prospers.

51. Manton, *Psalm 119*, 6:99.

52. Manton, *Psalm 119*, 6:100. Manton believes that "meditation is the mother and nurse of knowledge and godliness, the great instrument in all the offices of grace." It helps the work of grace upon the understanding: "Continual meditation maketh religious thoughts actual and present." Further, it helps the work of grace on the affections: "Serious meditation hath this advantage, that it doth make the object present, and as it were sensible." These "ponderous thoughts" become "bellows that kindle and inflame the affections." Finally, it helps the work of grace on the life: "It maketh the heavenly life more easy, more sweet, more orderly and prudent." *Sermons on Genesis 24:63*, 17:274–77.

53. Manton, *Psalm 119*, 6:106. "Among scholars, those whose knowledge is confined to books, if they have not the books always before them, readily discover their ignorance; in like manner, if we do not imbibe the doctrine of God, and are well acquainted with it, Satan will easily surprise and entangle us in his meshes." Calvin, *Commentary on the Book of Psalms*, 4:409.

54. Manton, *Psalm 119*, 6:106.

55. "When the Word is hidden in the heart, the life shall be hidden from sin." Spurgeon, *Golden Alphabet*, 48.

against temptations by furnishing us the strength required to mortify the flesh. It comforts us in troubles and afflictions because it possesses a remedy for every malady. Finally, it seasons our conversation with others.[56]

Conclusion

"Mine eyes prevent the night watches, that I might meditate in thy word" (Ps. 119:148). Scripture meditation begins in the mind, embraces the affections, and expresses itself in the will. The Holy Spirit uses this faculty-focused meditation to span the gap between the head and the heart, thereby producing *practical* knowledge—the cause of all godliness. Manton declares, "Meditation is not a flourishing of the wit, that we may please the fancy by playing with divine truths…but a serious inculcation of them upon the heart, that we may urge it to practice."[57]

The enjoyment of the eternal God is our "end and scope."[58] Therefore, we must set eternal things before us—on the one side there are "eternal joys" and "solid godliness," while on the other side there are "eternal torments" and "vain pleasures." Having considered these things, we must take the eternal God as our portion, seeking to "do all things from eternal principles to eternal ends."[59] Then, we must apply Scripture to our lives. Whether it is the curses and commands of the law or the comforts of the gospel, we must appropriate them by faith. To sum up, we must "eat the word." We believe that God is its author and that its precepts and promises are directed at us. When we hear God's precepts in fear, the result is obedience, and when we hear God's promises in faith, the result is hope. Every recorded work of God serves to strengthen our faith, while every recorded promise of God serves to strengthen our hope.

---

56. Manton, *Psalm 119*, 6:101–2.

57. Manton, *Psalm 119*, 6:138. For some insight into Manton's emphasis on solitude, see Crawford Gribben, "Thomas Manton and the Spirituality of Solitude," *Eusebeia: The Bulletin of the Jonathan Edwards Centre for Reformed Spirituality* 6 (Spring 2007): 21–23.

58. Manton, *Psalm 119*, 7:399.

59. Manton, *Psalm 119*, 7:400.

Our minds are restless, and thus we are always thinking of something. For Manton, the issue is whether our thoughts are heavenly or worldly. He maintains, "The more the heart is replenished with holy meditation, the less will it be pestered with worldly and carnal thoughts." It will "inflame and enkindle" our affections after heavenly things.[60]

---

60. Manton, *Psalm 119*, 7:481.

Chapter 16

Delighting

As we have seen, God's Word is the instrument of all the good that He communicates to us.[1] It is a manifesting light by which He imparts heavenly wisdom to us. It is a directing light by which He leads us in the way of salvation. It is a quickening light by which He renews our spiritual vitality. And it is a comforting light by which He strengthens us in times of difficulty. That being the case, we ought to "busy ourselves" with it.[2] For Manton, this "busying" entails meditating on, delighting in, and obeying God's Word per the psalmist's proclamation in Psalm 119:47–48, "And I will delight myself in thy commandments, which I have loved. My hands also will I lift up unto thy commandments, which I have loved; and I will meditate in thy statutes."

When we meditate on God's Word, we seek to reflect its light into our souls. We digest it; that is, we bring its truths to remembrance and consider it until it is impressed "upon the heart."[3] When God's Word is internalized in this way, it grips our affections. Our love is set on it, meaning we desire it and delight in it. "I will delight myself in thy statutes," declares the psalmist (Ps. 119:16).[4] God's Word is, according to Manton, "one of the greatest enjoyments [we] have on this side of

---

1. Manton, *Psalm 119*, 6:148. Manton adds, "It is the property of a gracious soul to delight in God's commandments." *Psalm 119*, 9:20. See Pss. 1:2; 112:1; Rom. 7:22.

2. Manton, *Psalm 119*, 7:433.

3. Manton, *Psalm 119*, 6:138.

4. For the psalmist's delight in God's Word, see Ps. 119:14, 16, 20, 24, 35, 38, 40, 47, 48, 70, 72, 77, 92, 97, 103, 113, 119, 127, 129, 131, 143, 159, 162, 163, 167, 174.

heaven, in the time of [our] absence from God."[5] This delight is real
because it depends not on changing circumstances but on an unchanging God. It is cordial because it fills the heart with serenity and peace.
It is great because "it doth ravish the heart." And it is pure because it is
fixed on God's promises.[6]

The Nature of Delight

Our delight in God's Word is the result of our esteem. Manton unpacks
what it means to esteem God's Word by explaining that there is a twofold act of judgment.[7] The first is that whereby we distinguish between
good and evil, and the second is that whereby we compare between
good and best. By the first act we approve of those things that are
good, but by the second act we judge what is best—the Word. Manton
makes it clear that this is not "a slight and superficial esteem, but such
as is deep and solid."[8]

How do we know if our esteem is "deep and solid"? First, we look
at its root. True esteem flows from "a vital principle of grace...a full
purpose of heart."[9] Second, we look at its object. True esteem does not
flow from "a temporal, natural, or carnal motive, but the moral goodness of the law"—that is to say, it values the Bible as "the pure and holy
word and will of God."[10] Third, we look at its influence. True esteem
has "a lively and effectual influence upon our hearts and ways." Manton
is careful to note that there is a liking that never engages the soul to
pursue that which it esteems. In marked contrast, true esteem produces
a "constant, habitual willingness" that compels us to do God's will with
"life, power, and earnestness."[11]

---

5. Manton, *Psalm 119*, 6:148.

6. Manton, *Psalm 119*, 6:224–26.

7. Manton, *Psalm 119*, 8:325.

8. Manton, *Psalm 119*, 8:325. See Matt. 13:20; Heb. 6:5.

9. Manton, *Psalm 119*, 8:326.

10. Manton, *Psalm 119*, 8:326.

11. Manton, *Psalm 119*, 8:326. Manton observes, "Many could be content with
God's law, so far as it doth not cross their carnal interest, or hinder their corrupt desires."
Psalm 119, 8:328. "My soul hath kept thy testimonies; and I love them exceedingly"
(Ps. 119:167). "It is not enough to keep the commandments," says Manton, "but we

The Cause of Delight

This deep and solid esteem takes root when we perceive the excellency of God's Word.[12] It is a clear Word in that it reveals God to us, a good Word in that it satisfies all our needs, a pure Word in that it reflects God's holiness, a sublime Word in that it contains glorious mysteries, and a sure Word in that it contains unfailing promises. Thus, we join with the psalmist in proclaiming, "I have rejoiced in the way of thy testimonies, as much as in all riches" (Ps. 119:14). Again, "I love thy commandments above gold; yea, above fine gold" (Ps. 119:127).

Everyone seeks for riches. What makes God's people unique is that they have discovered that true riches reside in God's Word.[13] We possess "a sweet sense of the goodness of it" in our souls; as a result, we "delight and rejoice in it above all things."[14] Because our minds are designed to find satisfaction in a "fit object" (i.e., truth), we experience "delectation" when we read God's Word.[15] Its truth is more sublime than other truths, and it is suitable to our greatest needs. "To every man that hath a conscience," says Manton, "it cannot but be very pleasing to hear of a way how he may come to the pardon of sins, and sound peace of conscience, solid perfection, and eternal glory."[16] God's Word offers such a suitable remedy for our sin that we should welcome it as we would a friend's counsel that rescues us from a great misery.[17] God's

---

must love them, and that obedience they require from us." *Psalm 119*, 9:233. He further states that without love, "our obedience is not sincere and acceptable." It breeds in us "a reverent fear of God's majesty, and a care to please him in all things." *Psalm 119*, 9:237. "Till sight be turned into love, it hath not such a powerful influence upon us." *Psalm 119*, 9:214.

12. Manton, *Psalm 119*, 9:202–4. See also 6:149–50; 7:263–64, 463–64; 9:21–22. God's Word is "good" (v. 39), "right" (v. 75), "faithful" (v. 86), and "true" (v. 160). It "endureth forever" (v. 160). It is the psalmist's "song" (v. 54), and "better than thousands of gold and silver" (v. 72).

13. Manton, *Psalm 119*, 6:133.

14. Manton, *Psalm 119*, 6:129.

15. Manton, *Psalm 119*, 6:130. See Proverbs 24:14. God's Word is the "chief" truth, "only" truth, "pure" truth, and "whole" truth. *Psalm 119*, 9:12–13.

16. Manton, *Psalm 119*, 6:130. See also 7:10.

17. Manton, *Psalm 119*, 7:7.

Word is His "love-letter" to us.[18] As such, it is our direction. It reveals evils so that we might see them and forsake them, and it reveals the "ready way to heaven" so that we might walk in it.[19] It is also our support: "One promise in the word of God," says Manton, "doth bear up the heart more than all the arguing and discourses of men."[20] Finally, it is our charter, containing "promises of eternal joy and blessedness," which make way for "strong consolation."[21]

The Intensity of Delight

"My soul breaketh for the longing that it hath unto thy judgments at all times" (Ps. 119:20). Here the psalmist reveals an essential property of delight in God's Word: an earnest and constant bent of heart to get more of it. Simply put, we cannot live without it.[22] This kind of delight is not "an outward receiving" or "a loose owning" of the Scripture as God's Word. It is not "a bare approbation" of Scripture's purity and holiness, nor is it "a pang or passionate delight" for Scripture that passes in a moment.[23] On the contrary, it is such a delight that causes us "to wait at wisdom's gates, to consult with the word upon all occasions, to read it, hear it, meditate on it as the greatest instrument of sanctification."[24] It is such a delight that makes us afraid to transgress it and makes us earnest "to do what it requireth in order to the glory of God and our own salvation."[25]

---

18. Manton, *Psalm 119*, 6:149. See also 6:191.

19. Manton, *Psalm 119*, 6:149. See 2 Peter 1:19.

20. Manton, *Psalm 119*, 6:150. See Ps. 119:50.

21. Manton, *Psalm 119*, 6:150. Manton explains that we love God's Word because "it is the charter of our hopes and the rule of our duty." To love it as "the charter of our hopes" is to love God's favor as found in "pardon of sins, peace of conscience, taking away the stony heart, and eternal life." To love it as "the rule of our duty" is to love holiness—"loving things as suitable to our necessities, and as suitable to our dispositions." *Psalm 119*, 8:315.

22. Manton, *Psalm 119*, 6:185.

23. Manton, *Psalm 119*, 8:483.

24. Manton, *Psalm 119*, 8:483.

25. Manton, *Psalm 119*, 8:484.

When we delight in God's Word with an earnest and constant bent of heart, it "draws us off from carnal vanities."[26] For Manton, we cure delight with delight—"delight in God's statutes is the cure of delight in worldly things." The reason for this is obvious: "love cannot lie idle, it must be occupied one way or another; either carried out to the contentments of the flesh, or else to holy things." Moreover, when we delight in God's Word with an earnest and constant bent of heart, it removes "the tediousness of religious exercises."[27] When it comes to "hunting, fowling, and fishing" and "our ordinary employments," we count the difficulty and hardship as nothing because we "delight in them." The same is true of spiritual duties. Delight "facilitates duties, and removes difficulties in working."[28]

Conclusion

According to Manton, all the affections depend on pleasure (delight) or pain (grief)—the first is proper to the soul; the second is proper to the body. "Delight, if not right set, of all the affections, is apt to degenerate."[29] We must, therefore, lay aside whatever disrupts our capacity to enjoy God's Word.[30] God provided the Israelites with manna to sustain them on their journey to Canaan. There was nothing wrong with the manna, yet they grew weary of it (Num. 11:5–6). Similarly, many of us grow weary of God's Word because we have dulled our appetite for it due to our close proximity to the world. In large part, this is a result of our failure to esteem God's Word rightly. If we love God, we will delight in His Word because it is the perfect representation of Him. If we love holiness, we will delight in God's Word because it is the rule to holiness. If we love happiness, we will delight in God's

---

26. Manton, *Psalm 119*, 6:150.

27. Manton, *Psalm 119*, 6:148. See also 6:186.

28. Manton, *Psalm 119*, 9:22.

29. Manton, *Psalm 119*, 6:151.

30. According to Manton, we cultivate this delight through means because we cannot delight in what we do not know. This implies that, in addition to reading and listening, we "confer of it" with others, for "what a man delighteth in he will be talking of." *Psalm 119*, 6:148.

Word because "it is the way that leadeth us to so blessed and glorious an estate." If we love Christ, we will delight in God's Word because it offers Him to us. If we love the new nature, we will delight in God's Word because it is the seed by which it is produced in us.[31]

31. Manton, *Psalm 119*, 9:22–23.

Chapter 17

Obeying

"And I will delight myself in thy commandments, which I have loved. My hands also will I lift up unto thy commandments, which I have loved; and I will meditate in thy statutes" (Ps. 119:47–48). Here the psalmist expresses his resolve to employ all his faculties with God's Word.[1] With his mind he will meditate on God's Word, and with his affections he will delight in God's Word. As a result, he will "lift up" his hands to obey God's Word. For Manton, the relationship between knowing, delighting, and obeying is pivotal. He is adamant that knowing and delighting without corresponding practice is absurd.[2] Apart from "the practice of holy obedience," knowing and delighting are but speculative exercises.[3] Manton warns that "a naked approbation" of the Bible is not enough. God's Word must have "a real dominion over and influence upon our practice."[4]

Manton's convictions in this regard are on full display throughout his sermon series on Psalm 119. An interesting case in point is his exposition of verse 63, in which the psalmist states, "I am a companion of all them that fear thee, and of them that keep thy precepts."[5] Based on this verse, Manton affirms that God's people are known

---

1. Manton, *Psalm 119*, 7:12.
2. Manton, *Psalm 119*, 7:13. See 1 John 3:18.
3. Manton, *Psalm 119*, 7:13.
4. Manton, *Psalm 119*, 7:18.
5. See also Ps. 119:74, 120, 161.

by two unmistakable marks—their "principle" (fear) and their "course" (obedience).[6]

A Principle: Fear

According to Manton, *natural* fear occurs when we perceive approaching evil or impending danger. This is an entirely natural reaction—an essential part of human nature. Why? We fear what threatens us, and, in response, we avoid what we fear. This is crucial to survival. From here Manton proceeds to identify a "double fear": *servile* ("which driveth us from God") and *filial* ("which draweth us to God").[7] George Swinnock makes the same distinction.[8] William Gurnall refers to these two as *slavish* fear and *holy* fear.[9] Stephen Charnock distinguishes between *bondage* fear and *reverential* fear.[10] These Puritans are affirming that there are two different ways of fearing God: a *good* way and a *bad* way.

This distinction is biblical. It is seen, for example, in the case of the Israelites when they are gathered at the foot of Mount Sinai.[11] They see the fire, smoke, and lightning, and they hear thunder. They are overwhelmed by this physical manifestation of God's glory and, as a result, are terrified. But Moses speaks to them, "*Fear* not: for God is come to prove you, and that his *fear* may be before your faces, that ye sin not" (Ex. 20:20, italics mine). In short, Moses tells the Israelites not to fear, but to fear. This apparent contradiction is resolved when we acknowledge that there are two kinds of fear. As John Bunyan writes, "Mark it, here are two fears: a fear forbidden and a fear commended."[12]

---

6. Manton, *Psalm 119*, 7:171.

7. Manton, *Psalm 119*, 7:172. See also 8:231.

8. Swinnock, *Works of George Swinnock*, 3:295.

9. Gurnall, *Christian in Complete Armour*, 1:119, 222, 263, 372–73; 2:579.

10. Charnock, *Existence and Attributes of God*, 1:27, 41, 98, 172, 231, 236, 254; 2:107–9.

11. For another example, see 1 Sam. 12:18–24.

12. John Bunyan, *A Treatise on the Fear of God* (1679; repr., Morgan, Pa.: Soli Deo Gloria, 1999), 29.

Servile Fear

According to Manton, servile fear is that "by which a man feareth God and hateth him, as a slave feareth his cruel master, whom he could wish dead, and himself rid of his service, and obeyeth by mere compulsion and constraint."[13] This occurs when we fear only the punishment of God. At Mount Sinai, the Israelites feared God because they viewed Him as a perceived threat; in other words, they regarded Him as hazardous to their well-being. Servile fear is merely concerned with self-preservation. Those who fear God in this manner "are not troubled for the offence done to God, but their own danger; not for sin, but merely the punishment."[14] For this reason, servile fear falls short of making any lasting impression on the soul. Stephen Charnock affirms, "Many men perform those duties that the law requires with the same sentiments that slaves perform their drudgery; and are constrained in their duties by no other considerations but those of the whip and cudgel. Since, therefore, they do it with reluctance, and secretly murmur while they seem to obey, they would be willing that both the command were recalled, and the master that commands them were in another world."[15] People actually desire the annihilation of what they fear will harm them. This means that ungodly fear is tantamount to desiring the annihilation of God, who is perceived as detrimental to their self-interest.[16] "Slavish fear hateth God for his holiness, and feareth him for his wrath; they wish his destruction, that there were no God."[17]

Filial Fear

For Manton, filial fear is that by which we approach God as children, meaning we "love him, and obey him, and cleave to him."[18] It is a "fear

---

13. Manton, *Psalm 119*, 7:172.

14. Manton, *Sermons on Romans 8*, 12:108.

15. Charnock, *Existence and Attributes of God*, 1:98.

16. Charnock, *Existence and Attributes of God*, 1:98–99. For examples, see Ex. 9:20–30; 2 Kings 17:25–41.

17. Manton, *Exposition of Jude*, 5:361.

18. Manton, *Psalm 119*, 7:172. For more on this subject, see Thomas Manton, *Sermon on Acts 10:34–35*, in Manton, *Works*, 18:411–12.

of reverence" that keeps us from offending Him and a "fear of caution"
that keeps us devoted to "the business of salvation with all possible
solicitude and care."[19] It does not arise out of a perception of God as
hazardous, but as glorious. In other words, it flows from our appreciation of God.[20] We possess a "sense of God's majesty and goodness."[21]
As William Gouge explains, "A son fears simply to offend or displease
his father: so as it is accompanied with love. A bond slave fears nothing
but the punishment of his offence; so as it is joined with hatred."[22] For
this reason, servile fear never makes a divorce between sin and the soul,
whereas filial fear does.[23] "The fear of the LORD is to hate evil" (Prov.
8:13). Filial fear results in "a careful endeavour to please God" and "a
careful avoiding of such things as offend the Majesty of God."[24]

A Course: Obedience

For Manton, the relationship between fearing God and obeying God
is crucial. We grow in holiness "as the fear of God doth more prevail in [our] hearts." He adds, "As the stream is dried up that wanteth
a fountain, so godliness ceaseth as the fear of God abateth."[25] But

---

19. Manton, *Psalm 119*, 7:173. For Manton, "The whole perfection of the Christian life is comprised in these two—believing God and fearing him, trusting in his
mercy and fearing his name; the one maketh us careful in avoiding sin, the other diligent to follow after righteousness; the one is a bridle from sin and temptations, the other
a spur to our duties." *Psalm 119*, 7:280–81.

20. "Familiarity with God breeds a holy awe of him." Spurgeon, *Golden Alphabet*,
225. For examples, see Gen. 22:12; 42:18; Ex. 3:6; 2 Sam. 6:9; 1 Kings 18:3; Neh. 1:11;
Job 1:1, 8–9; Acts 9:31; 10:2, 22; Phil. 2:12; Heb. 11:7; 1 Peter 1:17.

21. Manton, *Psalm 119*, 7:173. Manton states, "It is not such a fear as driveth us
from God (Genesis 3:5), but bringeth us to him, and keepeth us with him." *Psalm 119*,
8:234.

22. William Gouge, *Of Domesticall Duties: Eight Treatises* (London, 1622), 9.

23. For examples, see Lev. 19:14, 32; 25:17, 36, 43; Josh. 24:14; 1 Sam. 12:24; Pss.
2:11; 112:1; Prov. 14:2; Eccl. 12:13; Acts 10:1–2, 35; Rom. 11:20; Eph. 5:21; Heb. 4:1;
12:28–29; Rev. 19:5.

24. Gouge, *Domesticall Duties*, 8. Manton comments, "There are three things that
will incline the soul to duty—the forcible principle is God's love, the mighty aid is
God's Spirit, the high aim is God's glory." *Psalm 119*, 4:233.

25. Manton, *Psalm 119*, 7:172. "The fear of God is the root or origin of all righteousness, and by dedicating our life to his service, we manifest that his fear dwells in

when the fear of God abounds in the soul, "it is the great excitement to obedience."[26] This deep awe of God on the soul causes us to perform spiritual duties "reverently and seriously," to regard all our "duties towards men," and to pursue the "business of our salvation" with "zeal and diligence."[27] Our obedience becomes universal; we do not content ourselves with a "partial reformation in outward things." It also becomes serious and settled, meaning we pursue it "with the greatest care."[28] In addition, the fear of God ensures that our obedience flows from "a right principle"—namely, faith and love.[29] For Manton, "faith begets love, and love obedience," and these are the "true principles of all Christian actions."[30] The fear of God also ensures that our obedience aims at "a right end"—namely, the glory of God.[31]

This kind of obedience is expressed in zeal.[32] The psalmist declares, "My zeal hath consumed me" (Ps. 119:139). "Great and pure zeal becomes those that have any affection for the word and for the ways of God," says Manton.[33] Its cause is "love to God and what belongs to God," while its object is "God's truth, worship, and servants."[34] It is seen

---

our hearts." Calvin, *Commentary on the Book of Psalms*, 4:448. Plumer observes, "There is a beautiful harmony and symmetry in Christian character. Fear makes the godly man sober; joy makes him lively; abhorrence of sin makes him cautious and watchful; love makes him serve willingly and give liberally; peace makes him tranquil; hope gives an anchor to his soul; faith in an omniscient God makes him serve not man, but his Maker; praise gives him songs in the night; and obedience makes him work righteousness with all diligence." *Psalms*, 1088.

26. Manton, *Psalm 119*, 7:173. "If our piety does not lead us to fear God, and keep his commandments, we may know that our profession is vain." Plumer, *Psalms*, 1049.

27. Manton, *Psalm 119*, 7:174.

28. Manton, *Psalm 119*, 7:13–14.

29. Manton, *Psalm 119*, 7:15.

30. Manton, *Psalm 119*, 7:15.

31. Manton, *Psalm 119*, 7:15. See 1 Cor. 10:31.

32. "Zeal is a passion, whose real character must be determined by the objects on which it is employed, and the principle by which it is directed. There is a true and a false zeal, differing as widely from each other, as an heavenly flame from the infernal fire." Bridges, *Psalm 119*, 366.

33. Manton, *Psalm 119*, 8:466.

34. Manton, *Psalm 119*, 8:468–69.

in commitment to duty and expressed in "holy grief and anger."[35] It leads us to resolve with the psalmist: "I have sworn, and I will perform it, that I will keep thy righteous judgments" (Ps. 119:106).[36] It also leads us to deal definitely with our sin.[37] "Sin dieth when it dieth in the affections," says Manton.[38] We hate sin because it is "contrary and repugnant" to the object of our love: God.

Conclusion

For Manton, the fear of God and His Word is foundational to our blessedness.[39] There are many who fear God's judgment and threatening, but this servile fear is not the result of a "gracious heart."[40] It "driveth" them from God's Word and is, therefore, the effect of legalism. In marked contrast, filial fear "draweth" us to God's Word because it is the fruit of holy love.[41] For Manton, this is the indissoluble link between meditating, delighting, and obeying. With the mind we perceive God's excellence, and with the affections we embrace it. And, then, we say with the psalmist, "My hands also will I lift up unto thy commandments" (Ps. 119:48). For Manton, such living "always in an admiration of his excellent majesty, a thankful sense of his goodness, and a regard to his eye and presence" is true blessedness.[42]

---

35. Manton, *Psalm 119*, 8:471. Manton believes "holy" zeal is different from "carnal" zeal because it is "accompanied with knowledge and discretion"; "mingled with compassion, that as we mind the glory of God, so we may pity deluded souls"; and "constant." *Psalm 119*, 8:472–74.

36. According to Manton, this kind of resolution is necessary because of our "backwardness," "fickleness," and "laziness." *Psalm 119*, 8:82–84. "Wherever the Spirit of God reigns, He excites this ardent zeal, which burns the hearts of the godly when they see the commandment of the Most High God accounted as a thing of naught." Calvin, *Commentary on the Book of Psalms*, 5:17.

37. Manton, *Psalm 119*, 8:331.

38. Manton, *Psalm 119*, 8:330.

39. Manton, *Psalm 119*, 7:175. See Prov. 28:14.

40. Manton, *Psalm 119*, 9:169.

41. Manton, *Psalm 119*, 9:169.

42. Manton, *Psalm 119*, 7:175. "The more reverence we have for the word of God the more joy we shall find in it." Henry, *Commentary on the Whole Bible*, 714.

Chapter 18

Prayer and Praise

Given his conviction that the instrument by which spiritual life is produced is faith, and that the instrument by which faith is "fed and increased" is God's Word, Manton commits himself to God's Word. He finds this patterned in the psalmist's resolve to "employ all his faculties" with God's Word.[1] With his mind he meditates on it, with his affections he delights in it, and with his hands he obeys it (Ps. 119:47–48). For Manton, these three—knowing, delighting, and obeying—constitute the essence of what it means to pursue God's Word. It is through this pursuit that the Holy Spirit nurtures faith and thus the enjoyment of God.

As God's Word is implanted through knowing, delighting, and obeying, it finds expression in our experience. The psalmist declares, "Accept, I beseech thee, the freewill offerings of my mouth, O LORD, and teach me thy judgments" (Ps. 119:108). He does not ask God to accept the freewill offerings of his hands ("legal sacrifices") but rather the freewill offerings of his mouth ("spiritual services").[2] Manton maintains that we are priests because we enjoy communion with Christ in His office of priest.[3] As such, we offer spiritual sacrifices (or services) to God. The most significant of these is a "thank-offering" whereby we present ourselves to Him for His "use and service."[4] Paul writes, "I

---

1. Manton, *Psalm 119*, 7:12.
2. Manton, *Psalm 119*, 8:106.
3. Manton, *Psalm 119*, 8:107. See 1 Peter 2:5, 9; Rev. 1:6.
4. Manton, *Psalm 119*, 8:108.

beseech you therefore, brethren, by the mercies of God, that ye present your bodies a living sacrifice, holy, acceptable unto God, which is your reasonable service" (Rom. 12:1). Here Paul is thinking in terms of the Old Testament burnt offerings. The Israelites were required to bring an animal without defect and offer it on the altar, where it was totally consumed. The sacrifice represented their complete consecration to God, and it was an act of thanksgiving. Paul calls us to do likewise—consecrate our lives to God as living sacrifices.

In addition to our lives, God requires two "great sacrifices."[5] The first is prayer: "Let my prayer be set forth before thee as incense; and the lifting up of my hands as the evening sacrifice" (Ps. 141:2). The second is praise: "I will freely sacrifice unto thee: I will praise thy name, O LORD; for it is good" (Ps. 54:6). According to Manton, our prayers and praises are "oblations" that we offer to God, either acknowledging "former mercies" or requesting "future deliverances." He adds, "These are the two duties which contain the substance of the ceremonies under the law, and are daily and constantly to be performed by us."[6]

Prayer

Manton, turning to prayer specifically, describes it as "a solemn preaching to ourselves, or a serious warming of our souls in our duty in the sight of God."[7] He offers his insights regarding the nature and content of prayer in his sermons on Psalm 119:145–46, in which the psalmist declares, "I cried with my whole heart; hear me, O LORD: I will keep thy statutes. I cried unto thee; save me, and I shall keep thy testimonies."[8]

---

5. Manton, *Psalm 119*, 8:108.

6. Manton, *Psalm 119*, 8:109.

7. Manton, *Psalm 119*, 8:204. We can view ordinances (such as prayer) as duties, privileges, and means of growth, for which we will give an account. Manton explains, "Some do not look upon them as duties, and so neglect them; others not as privileges, and so do not prize them, are not joyful in the house of prayer; others not as means, and so rest in the bear performance, without looking after the fruits to be had thereby; others not as talents, and so are more indifferent whether they get good by them, yea or no; But when all these are regarded, we act best in any service or ordinance." *Psalm 119*, 9:46.

8. The subject of prayer emerges frequently in Manton's works. See *Sermon on Isaiah 43:22*, 15:297–305; *Sermons on 1 Thessalonians 5:17*, 17:493–504; *Sermons on*

How We Pray

The psalmist cries with his "whole heart." Elsewhere, he declares, "I intreated thy favour with my whole heart: be merciful unto me according to thy word" (Ps. 119:58).[9] For Manton, this mention of the heart confirms that prayer is not merely a work of the understanding but of "faith, love, fear, zeal, hatred of sin, temperance, patience, and other virtues, which do bend the heart towards God, and draw it off from other things."[10] When the heart is thus engaged, we cry out to God.[11]

The psalmist's cry is, first, an "earnestness of the affection," meaning it is not chiefly external but internal.[12] Manton states, "It lieth not in the lifting up of the external voice, or the agitation of the bodily spirits, but the serious bent and frame of the spirit."[13] Most people are careless in this regard because they have "no feeling of their wants."[14] When we perceive the seriousness of our sin, we become poor in spirit. The result is godly sorrow—mourning for sin. These two naturally lead to meekness—an acknowledgment that anything short of God's judgment is a mercy. This, in turn, leads to an earnest and constant desire for the righteousness of God (Matt. 5:3–8).[15] The psalmist's crying, for Manton, points to his "vehemency and earnestness" as opposed to

2 Samuel 7:27, 18:62–63. For a full treatment, see *Practical Exposition of the Lord's Prayer*, 1:4–254.

9. "Whatever blessings the saints may plead for in prayer, their opening argument must be the free and unmerited grace of God." Calvin, *Commentary on the Book of Psalms*, 5:27.

10. Manton, *Psalm 119*, 9:43.

11. "The new creature is not lifeless and senseless, but cries mightily to God." Plumer, *Psalms*, 1048.

12. Manton writes, "Draw nigh doth chiefly imply humble and fervorous addresses; when you come naked to God, as the rich man that will clothe you; hungry to God, as the bountiful man that will feed you; sick to God, as the physician that will cure you; as servants to your Lord, as disciples to your master, as blind to the light, as cold to the fire, &c. The creatures addresses are best when they begin in want and end in hope." *Exposition of James*, 4:369.

13. Manton, *Psalm 119*, 9:38.

14. Manton, *Psalm 119*, 9:39–40. For Manton's insights regarding our words, thoughts, and affections in prayer, see *Practical Exposition of the Lord's Prayer*, 1:32–38.

15. Manton, *Psalm 119*, 9:39–40.

"careless formality and deadness."[16] He is aware of his spiritual condition, and therefore he complains directly to God.[17] This is one of the reasons that meditation is so important to prayer: "What we take in by the word we digest by meditation, and let out by prayer. These three duties help one another. What is the reason men have such a barren, dry, and sapless spirit in their prayers? It is for want of exercising themselves in holy thoughts."[18]

The psalmist's cry is, second, "stirred up by the Spirit."[19] By way of explanation, Manton appeals to Paul's words in Romans 8:26–27: "Likewise the Spirit also helpeth our infirmities: for we know not what we should pray for as we ought: but the Spirit itself maketh intercession for us with groaning which cannot be uttered. And he that searcheth the hearts knoweth what is the mind of the Spirit, because he maketh intercession for the saints according to the will of God." Here Paul affirms that "we do not know what we should pray for as we ought."[20] He proceeds to assure us that the Holy Spirit "helpeth our infirmities." The verb translated as *help* conveys the idea of a man who is carrying a heavy load. He soon realizes it is beyond his strength. He is unable to carry it on his own, and it is weighing him down. Thankfully, another man comes alongside to help bear the load. Similarly, the Holy Spirit helps us by bearing the load. Manton comments, "We cannot look aright to the blessed Father, but we must look to him through the blessed Son, and we cannot look upon the Son but through the blessed Spirit."[21] It is the Holy Spirit who "maketh intercession for us with groaning which cannot be uttered."[22] He does not remove our

---

16. Manton, *Psalm 119*, 9:37.

17. Manton, *Psalm 119*, 9:37.

18. Manton, *Psalm 119*, 6:142. "It is instructive to find meditation so constantly connected with fervent prayer: it is the fuel which sustains the flame." Spurgeon, *Golden Alphabet*, 263.

19. Manton, *Psalm 119*, 9:38.

20. Manton notes, "We cannot speak of God without the Spirit, much less to God." *Sermons on Romans 8*, 12:235.

21. Manton, *Sermons on Romans 8*, 12:235.

22. There are two views among Reformed scholars as to the meaning of these words. (1) It refers to the Holy Spirit's teaching. Some struggle with the idea that the

weakness, but makes our prayers intelligible. The Father searches our hearts, and hears this groaning, and He hears the Holy Spirit's clear intention that certain decisions and circumstances come about in the exact way that will bring the most glory to God.[23] In addition, the Holy Spirit helps us in a way of "gifts," meaning He enables us to "put [our] meaning in apt words." He also helps in a way of "graces," meaning He "moves and assists" us so that we pray for the right matter in the right manner.[24]

What We Pray

"I cried unto thee; save me." In many ways, this request encapsulates all our prayers.[25] God's people are those who have made Him their portion; as a result, "they earnestly and constantly, above all things, desire

---

Holy Spirit prays for believers, because they believe such a notion undermines the need for Christ's intercessory work. For this reason, they interpret this verse along the same lines as Zechariah 12:10; namely, the Holy Spirit creates all genuine prayer. "It is his function to intercede for us, to pray in us, i.e., to make our prayers. He, as it were, writes our petitions in the heart, we offer them; he incites a good matter, we express it. That prayer which we are to believe will be accepted, is the work of the Holy Ghost; it is his voice, motion, operation, and so his prayer. Therefore when we pray he is said to pray, and our groans are called his, and our design and intent in prayer his meaning… (Romans 8:26–27)." David Clarkson, *The Works of David Clarkson* (1864–1865; repr., Edinburgh: Banner of Truth, 1988), 1:207. (2) It refers to the Holy Spirit's interceding. The phrase *Spirit himself* reveals that it is the Holy Spirit who is interceding. The verb *intercede* means to appeal or petition. It is accompanied by the preposition *for*, which means "for the benefit of another." The intercession consists of unutterable groaning. This is not vocal prayer.

23. Manton, *Exposition of James*, 4:469.

24. Manton, *Exposition of Jude*, 5:337–41. What does the Holy Spirit do in our prayers? (1) "He directeth and ordereth our requests so as they may suit with our great end, which is the enjoyment of God." This is necessary because we are preoccupied with the physical rather than the spiritual, and therefore we seek "the conveniences of the natural life rather than the enjoyment of the world to come." (2) "He quickeneth and enliveneth our desires in prayer." Our hearts are often "flat and dead." The Holy Spirit produces "lively motions" and "strong desires" whereby we cry out to God. (3) "He encourageth and emboldeneth us to come to God as a father." We come with "child-like confidence" and "child-like reverence." *Sermons on Romans 8*, 12:233–34.

25. "This is a golden prayer, as precious as it is short." Spurgeon, *Golden Alphabet*, 180.

his favor."[26] Manton remarks, "One good look from God the children of God prefer above all the world. All the earthly things cannot please them so much as a smile from God, nor put such gladness in their hearts."[27]

We prize God's favor because we feel our true misery. "I have declared my ways," confesses the psalmist (Ps. 119:26). We tell God how we are doing. We tell Him about the nature of our affairs and the condition of our hearts. We tell Him about our hopes, struggles, and distresses. We tell Him about our sins and temptations.[28] This is an "act of holy friendship" whereby we acquaint God with our "whole state."[29] It is an "act of spiritual contrition or brokenness of heart."[30] Everyone prays according to his perceived needs. As God's people, we possess a deeper sense of our sin, which is "the cause of all trouble." This compels us to seek "the favor of God and the grace of God" above all else.[31]

"But let him ask in faith, nothing wavering" (James 1:6). To pray in faith is to believe that there is a God (Heb. 11:6) who can accomplish all He desires (Eph. 3:20) because He is omnipotent as well as omniscient. It is to believe that God accepts our persons and prayers in Christ (Eph. 1:6).[32] And it is to pray according to God's will. Manton is adamant that faith is not the confidence that anything can happen but rather the confidence that what God has promised will happen. "And this is the confidence that we have in him, that, if we ask any thing according to his will, he heareth us" (1 John 5:14). John's statement means there are essentially three categories of prayer. First, there

---

26. Manton, *Psalm 119*, 7:119.

27. Manton, *Psalm 119*, 7:119.

28. Manton, *Psalm 119*, 6:243–45.

29. Manton, *Psalm 119*, 6:244.

30. Manton, *Psalm 119*, 6:245. "Sin is no light trouble to the man of God. Mercy, therefore, is to him no common blessing." Bridges, *Psalm 119*, 200.

31. Manton, *Psalm 119*, 7:121. Manton adds, "They that have a due sense of things upon their hearts will do so; that is to say, that have a sense of their own weakness, the evil of sin, and the comfort of perseverance in obedience." *Psalm 119*, 8:203. "The great error of most who profess the true religion is that they do not make enough of it. They do not habitually feel that God's favor is enough to compensate for all losses." Plumer, *Psalms*, 1067.

32. Manton, *Life of Faith*, 15:146–47.

are prayers that rest on specific promises and commands in God's Word (e.g., James 1:5). Second, there are prayers that rest on general promises and commands in God's Word (e.g., Matt. 6:33). Third, there are prayers that depart from God's Word (e.g., James 4:3). Requests that move beyond God's promises and commands are of the flesh, not the Spirit. All told, therefore, we must pray according to God's Word—not without a promise and not against a command.[33] Manton remarks, "The kind of God's answer must be referred to his own will, in all things for which we are not to pray absolutely."[34] Again, "Keep to the rule of prayer, ask the things that are agreeable to God's will and conducible to his glory; and fit for us to receive in our station, and then though they be ever so difficult, ever so many in number, ever so presently needed, we are confident we shall have the petitions we ask."[35]

Mercifully, God answers our prayers. At times He grants the exact mercy we request.[36] At times He does not grant the exact mercy we request, but He does impart "spiritual manifestations to the soul" for our encouragement. In other words, He gives us the light of His countenance along with "special discoveries" of His love and support until such time as He decides to bestow the mercy we request.[37] At other times, He does not grant the mercy we request but "another thing that is as good, or better for the party that prayeth."[38]

---

33. Manton, *Sermons on Romans 8*, 12:255. That means, in the words of John Calvin, "Faith grounded upon the Word is the mother of right prayer." *Institutes of the Christian Religion*, in *The Library of Christian Classics*, ed. J. T. McNeill (Philadelphia: Westminster Press, 1960), 3.20.27. "The more intimately we converse with the Word of God, and the more we dwell upon it in our thoughts, the better able we shall be to speak to God." Henry, *Commentary on the Whole Bible*, 713.

34. Manton, *Psalm 119*, 9:52.

35. Manton, *Life of Faith*, 15:148. Elsewhere Manton writes, "Consider, there is not a change in God, but a change in us, wrought by prayer. It is neither to give information to God, that he may know our meaning, nor to move him and persuade him to be willing by our much speaking, but only to raise up our own faith and hope towards God." *Lord's Prayer*, 1:29.

36. Manton, *Psalm 119*, 9:50.

37. Manton, *Psalm 119*, 9:50.

38. Manton, *Psalm 119*, 9:51.

Praise

Having considered prayer, we turn to praise: "Seven times a day do I praise thee because of thy righteous judgments" (Ps. 119:164). The psalmist praises God because of His "righteous judgments."[39] God's righteousness refers to "the whole rectitude and perfection" of His nature, meaning He always acts as becomes "such a pure, holy, and infinite being."[40] It is exercised in two principal ways. First, as Lord, His righteousness is "the absolute and free motion of his own will concerning the estate of all creatures."[41] He is wholly arbitrary, meaning He does not will things because they are just, but they are just because He wills them. Second, as Judge, His righteousness consists "in giving all their due according to his law."[42] He determines our duty and establishes rewards and punishments based on our obedience and disobedience; moreover, He renders unto all according to their works.[43]

Since God is righteous, then "all that comes from him is righteous."[44] In the context, this includes His judgments. For Manton, this expression specifically refers to "the dispensations of his providence" in "promises and threatenings fulfilled."[45] We praise God, therefore, for His righteous government of the world. In seasons of prosperity, we praise Him for His favors and the fulfillment of His promises to us. In seasons of adversity, we praise Him because we see His "hand…working for good."[46]

How We Praise

"Seven times a day do I praise thee."[47] The psalmist's "habit of thankfulness" reveals a heart "deeply affected with the Lord's excellencies and

---

39. See also Ps. 119:62, 137.
40. Manton, *Psalm 119*, 8:438.
41. Manton, *Psalm 119*, 8:438.
42. Manton, *Psalm 119*, 8:439.
43. Manton, *Psalm 119*, 8:440.
44. Manton, *Psalm 119*, 8:449.
45. Manton, *Psalm 119*, 9:190.
46. Manton, *Psalm 119*, 9:196.
47. According to Manton, "Seven is used for many." *Psalm 119*, 9:190. See Lev. 27:18; Prov. 24:16; 26:25; 1 Sam. 2:5.

mercies."[48] His praise flows from him "as water boileth and bubbleth up out of a fountain."[49] For Manton, praise is the fruit of faith and love. "Unless these praises flow from a believing, loving soul, they are but an empty prattle and a vain sound."[50] Faith sets God's power before us so that we behold Him "who liveth and reigneth forever, dispensing all things powerfully, according to his own will," whereas love sets God's goodness before us so that our hearts are enlarged toward Him. When these two graces prevail in the heart, the result is praise.

When we praise God, we acknowledge His "virtues, benefits, and perfections."[51] We wonder at His *being*. What manner of God is this? He knows no bounds, no beginning, no succession, and no addition. He is from everlasting to everlasting. He is the cause and original of all things. He is what He is in one indivisible point of eternity. We wonder at God's *attributes*. We admire His holiness: "Behold, he put no trust in his servants; and his angels he charged with folly" (Job 4:18). We admire His wisdom: "O the depth of the riches both of the wisdom and knowledge of God" (Rom. 11:33). We admire His love: "Behold, what manner of love the Father hath bestowed upon us" (1 John 3:1). We admire His power: "Who is a strong LORD like unto thee?" (Ps. 89:8). We wonder at God's *works*. "O LORD, how manifold are thy works!" (Ps. 104:24). Creation is marvelous and mysterious (Pss. 19:1; 104:24). Providence is full of curiosities and mysteries (Ps. 77:19). But redemption is God's masterpiece—a work into which the angels desire to look (1 Peter 1:12).

Why We Praise

For Manton, praise is a *necessary* duty. He declares, "God is continually beneficial to us, blessing and delivering his people every day, and by new mercies giveth us new matter of praise and thanksgiving."[52] He has "dealt well" with us (Ps. 119:65). He has been patient in bearing

---

48. Manton, *Psalm 119*, 9:193.
49. Manton, *Psalm 119*, 9:245.
50. Manton, *Psalm 119*, 9:191.
51. Manton, *Psalm 119*, 9:191.
52. Manton, *Psalm 119*, 7:161. See Ps. 68:19.

with us, hearing us, forgiving us, and keeping us. "What supplies and supports we have had, what visits of love, warnings, awakenings of heart!"[53]

Praise is, second, a *profitable* duty. It is profitable to faith in that it provides "matter of trust" by representing God to us "as a storehouse of all good things, and a sure foundation for dependence."[54] "Faith and praise live and die together," says Manton, "if there be faith, there will be praise; and if there be praise, there will be faith." It is also profitable to love: "Praise and thanksgiving is an act of love, and then it cherisheth and feedeth love."[55]

Praise is, third, a *pleasant* duty. "That which truly exhilarateth the soul, begets upon us a solid impression of God's love, that is the true pleasure."[56] Praising God is "good and profitable," "pleasant and delightful," and "comely and honorable."[57] Manton stresses the fact that praise is "our reward rather than our work, the heaven that we have upon earth." There is "nothing so fit to cheer up the spirit as to remember what a God we have in Christ."[58]

Praise is, fourth, an *honorable* duty. It is the "employment of angels" and our great honor "to be heralds to proclaim the Lord's glory."[59] Manton argues that "the principal end for which a man should live and desire life is to praise and glorify God."[60]

Conclusion

Under the law, God required the Israelites to offer their sacrifices with "brokenness of heart."[61] "The sacrifices of God are a broken spirit: a broken and a contrite heart, O God, thou wilt not despise" (Ps. 51:17). Likewise, we are to approach God in prayer and praise with a

---

53. Manton, *Psalm 119*, 7:161.
54. Manton, *Psalm 119*, 7:162.
55. Manton, *Psalm 119*, 7:200.
56. Manton, *Psalm 119*, 7:164.
57. Manton, *Psalm 119*, 9:192. See Pss. 50:23; 135:3; Eph. 1:12.
58. Manton, *Psalm 119*, 9:192. See Ps. 42:4.
59. Manton, *Psalm 119*, 9:193.
60. Manton, *Psalm 119*, 9:293.
61. Manton, *Psalm 119*, 8:109.

"sensibleness" of our spiritual poverty. In short, "we pray because we need God, and we praise him because we love him."[62] Secondly, under the law, God required the Israelites to offer their sacrifices with "an eyeing of the Redeemer."[63] For this reason, they placed their hands on the animal's head, thereby identifying their sins with it. This simple act pointed to Christ, who bore His people's sins. When we offer our sacrifices of prayer and praise, we do so through Christ, who "hath given himself for us an offering and a sacrifice to God for a sweetsmelling savour" (Eph. 5:2). Finally, under the law, God required the Israelites to offer their sacrifices with "a renewing of the covenant."[64] "Gather my saints together unto me; those that have made a covenant with me by sacrifice" (Ps. 50:5). Similarly, in our prayers and praises we devote ourselves afresh to God's service.

Prayer and praise are, for Manton, the believer's greatest privileges. The "Spirit of bondage" produces terror as we see ourselves as God sees us—sinful sinners. But the "Spirit of adoption" eases terror by leading us to Christ, in whom we find forgiveness (Rom. 8:15). Because of Christ, we approach God as our reconciled Father. He is not a terrifying God but a loving God; He is not a condemning God but a pardoning God; He is not a threatening God but an accepting God. Our peace with God is such that He loves us as if we had never been the object of His wrath, and thus we cry, "Abba, Father."[65]

---

62. Manton, *Psalm 119*, 7:162.
63. Manton, *Psalm 119*, 8:109.
64. Manton, *Psalm 119*, 8:110.
65. Manton, *Sermons on Romans 8*, 12:101–11.

Chapter 19

Suffering

God enjoyed is our blessedness. We grow in our enjoyment of Him as we are conformed to His likeness. We are conformed to His likeness as He impresses His greatness and goodness on us by means of His Word—a manifesting, directing, quickening, and comforting light. Given the sufficiency of God's Word to communicate blessedness to us, we devote ourselves to it by meditating on it, delighting in it, and obeying it. This devotion finds verbal expression in prayer and praise. For Manton, this is the spiritual life—the essence of what it means to commune with God.

While Manton believes that such communion is our normative experience as we pursue God in His Word, he maintains that it is a heightened experience when suffering. "I am afflicted very much" (Ps. 119:107).[1] Manton views the psalmist's affliction as a "special thinking," "special hearing," and "special awakening" time.[2] Above all else, it is a special season in which the blessed God speaks to His people by His Word.[3]

---

1. See also Ps. 119:50, 67, 71, 75, 92, 153.

2. Manton, *Psalm 119*, 7:256–57. Manton states, "The judgment of the saints and the judgment of the world about afflictions are far different; they have different principles—the spirit of the world, and the Spirit of God; they have different lights and rules—that of faith and that of sense." *Exposition of James*, 4:429.

3. There is no greater joy for the believer than fellowship with God. And that is how God promotes His people's happiness through suffering. Thomas Watson remarks, "The magnet of mercy does not draw us so near to God as the cords of affliction....

The Author

Manton makes it clear that God is the author of affliction.[4] Admittedly, this is a difficult truth to get our minds around. "We say we deserve nothing but evil from [God's] hands," observes Manton, "but yet are maddened like wild bulls in a net when the goad is in our sides."[5] It is important, therefore, for us to ponder the psalmist's assertion: "I know, O LORD, that thy judgments are right, and that thou in faithfulness hast afflicted me" (Ps. 119:75).

First, the psalmist says that God's "judgments are right." By "judgments" he means the passages of God's providence.[6] Manton clarifies that there is no "vindictive wrath" in God's judgments; rather, they are the means by which God corrects and humbles His people.[7] His judgments are right as to their *cause*: He never afflicts us above what we deserve. They are right as to their *measure*: He never afflicts us above what we can bear. And they are right as to their *end*: He afflicts us to accomplish His purposes for us.[8]

Second, the psalmist says that God afflicts us "in faithfulness." His point is that affliction is necessary precisely because God is faithful. He has engaged Himself to use all means that contribute to our eternal welfare.[9] Suffering, therefore, is not an indication of God's displeasure with us or rejection of us, but of His ownership of us.[10] Because our

---

Thus affliction makes us happy, in bringing us nearer to God." *All Things of Good; or, A Divine Cordial* (1663; repr., Edinburgh: Banner of Truth, 1994), 31.

4. Manton, *Psalm 119*, 7:28. See Heb. 12:5–6. For Manton, the author of affliction is God, while the meritorious cause is our sin and the final cause is our repentance. *Psalm 119*, 7:234. For more on this, see Swinnock, *Works of George Swinnock*, 2:82–83, 111; Charnock, *Existence and Attributes of God*, 2:309–10, 451–52.

5. Manton, *Psalm 119*, 7:234.

6. Manton, *Psalm 119*, 7:288. "This is a great stay to the soul in time of trouble. When we are sorely afflicted, and cannot see the reason for the dispensation, we may fall back upon this most certain fact, that God is righteous, and His dealings with us are righteous too." Spurgeon, *Golden Alphabet*, 250.

7. Manton, *Psalm 119*, 7:288–89. See 1 Peter 4:17.

8. Manton, *Psalm 119*, 7:289.

9. Manton, *Psalm 119*, 7:296.

10. Manton, *Psalm 119*, 7:298.

sanctification and glorification are for our eternal good, He designs all His judgments accordingly.[11]

To persevere through affliction, we must take to heart the righteousness and faithfulness of God in His providential dealings. We require "clearness of apprehension" and "firmness of persuasion."[12] It is not enough that we avoid murmuring when God afflicts us; instead, we must see His love and faithfulness in it.[13] God is faithful in all His dealings with us, even though we are often unable to comprehend His reasoning.[14] Therefore, we confess our ignorance and fix our eyes on Him. He is sovereign; thus His control is absolute. He is wise; thus His plan is perfect. He is incomprehensible; thus His providence is inscrutable. While not always understanding God's ways with us, we are certain that He is in control. "When all is hard and sharp to sense," says Manton, "faith can see all is for our profit, for our good."[15]

The Need

As mentioned, God afflicts His people for the purpose of sanctifying us—"that we might be partakers of his holiness" (Heb. 12:10).[16] This means that suffering is ultimately for our good.[17] Manton recognizes that this assertion is "a paradox to vulgar sense," adding, "the children of God can scarcely subscribe to the truth of it."[18] The reason for our hesitancy oftentimes arises from our misunderstanding of the nature of the *good* that is in view. We tend to define good according to what we want instead of what we need, what makes us happy instead of what

---

11. Manton, *Psalm 119*, 7:289–90. "When the Lord's painful work separates us from our sin, weans us from the world, and brings us nearer to himself, what remains for us, but thankfully to acknowledge his righteousness and truth?" Bridges, *Psalm 119*, 194.

12. Manton, *Psalm 119*, 7:290.

13. Manton, *Psalm 119*, 7:292. "It is a genuine evidence of true godliness, when, although plunged into the deepest afflictions, we yet cease not to submit ourselves to God." Calvin, *Commentary on the Book of Psalms*, 4:464.

14. Manton, *Psalm 119*, 7:293.

15. Manton, *Psalm 119*, 7:293.

16. Manton, *Psalm 119*, 7:28.

17. Manton, *Psalm 119*, 6:209–11. See also 6:413–18.

18. Manton, *Psalm 119*, 7:251.

makes us holy, what is visible instead of what is invisible, what is temporal instead of what is eternal, what is in the interest of the flesh rather than what is in the interest of the soul. We little regard holiness and little value blessedness; therefore, we resent the means to both.

By way of amplification, Manton appeals to Paul's testimony in Romans 8:28: "And we know that all things work together for good to them that love God, to them who are the called according to his purpose." On the basis of this verse, he clarifies the meaning of *good*.[19] First, this "good is not to be determined by our fancies and conceits, but by the wisdom of God." God sees "all things by one infinite act of understanding, but we judge according to present appearances." Second, this "good is to be determined by its respect to the chief good or true happiness." In a word, it increases "grace and holiness" so that "we enjoy God more surely." Third, this "good is not to be determined by the interest of the flesh, but the welfare of our souls." We do not judge our circumstances according to our "outward enjoyments" or "worldly comforts," but according to our "improvement of grace." Fourth, this "good is not to be determined by present feeling, but by the judgment of faith." Affliction is never pleasant to natural sense, nor is the fruit of affliction always evident to spiritual sense; but we do not determine what is good "by feeling, but by faith." Suffering is good because "it keepeth us from greater evils." In a word, it takes nothing from us but our sin.[20]

The Use

Related to the above, Manton affirms that affliction is "medicinal."[21] The cross of Christ changes the nature of affliction from "a destructive

---

19. Manton provides a similar explanation of *good* in *Transfiguration of Christ*, 1:379–82.

20. Manton, *Psalm 119*, 7:252–54. See also 8:254–57. Manton notes, "It is evil as it doth deprive us of our natural comforts, pleasure, gain, honor; but it is good as these may be recompensed with better pleasures, richer gain, and greater honor. There is more pleasure in holiness than there can be pain and trouble in affliction." *Psalm 119*, 7:256.

21. Manton, *Psalm 119*, 7:28.

punishment" to "a medicinal dispensation."[22] God uses it to change us "from vanity to seriousness, from error to truth, from stubbornness to teachfulness, from pride to modesty."[23] The psalmist declares, "Before I was afflicted I went astray: but now have I kept thy word" (Ps. 119:67).[24] We possess a "straying nature," which is "apt to turn out of the way that leadeth to God and to true happiness."[25] At times, we stray as a result of ignorance; at other times, we stray "out of perverseness of inclination."[26] This propensity to straying is heightened in seasons of prosperity. Manton has no issue with prosperity in itself but rather with our tendency to abuse it. Weakness and carelessness abound when all is well, and God must send affliction "to break us and bring us into order."[27]

Manton is careful to note that the nature of the affliction always corresponds to the nature of our wandering. He affirms, "Every cure

---

22. Manton, *Psalm 119*, 7:223. According to Thomas Watson, there are two kinds of providence: that which God overrules for good on behalf of the godly and that which God overrules for evil on behalf of the ungodly. In the case of the former, "All the various dealings of God with his children do by a special providence turn to their good." Watson, *All Things for Good*, 11. This is an excellent treatment of the subject. For another, see John Flavel, *Divine Conduct; or, The Mystery of Providence: A Treatise upon Psalm 57:2*, in *Works of John Flavel*, 4:339–497. Swinnock sees a clear difference between "'the punishments God inflicts on sinners' and 'the afflictions he brings on saints.'" *Works of George Swinnock*, 2:127. They differ in manner. God punishes His enemies with joy whereas He afflicts His children with compassion. They differ in measure. God punishes His enemies with no regard for what they can endure whereas He afflicts His children according to what they are able to suffer. They differ in end. God punishes His enemies to satisfy His offended judgment whereas He afflicts His children to sanctify their polluted hearts. In a word, God governs all things (including evil) for the welfare of His people.

23. Manton, *Psalm 119*, 7:223. "It is a blessed thing when our trials cure our earnest love for things that perish, and whet our appetites for divine comforts." Plumer, *Psalms*, 1057.

24. See also Ps. 119:71.

25. Manton, *Psalm 119*, 7:223. See Isa. 53:6.

26. Manton, *Psalm 119*, 7:224. Manton adds, "We have hearts that love to wander; we love shift and change, though it be for the worse."

27. Manton, *Psalm 119*, 7:224. "Prosperity is the unhappy occasion of much iniquity; it makes people conceited of themselves, indulgent of the flesh, forgetful of God, in love with the world, and deaf to the reproofs of the Word." Henry, *Commentary on the Whole Bible*, 709. "Often our trials act as a thorn-hedge to keep us in the good pasture; but our prosperity is a gap through which we go astray." Spurgeon, *Golden Alphabet*, 150.

will not fit every humor; all will not work alike upon all."[28] He believes there are three "impure fountains" that give rise to wandering, as identified in 1 John 2:16: "For all that is in the world, the lust of the flesh, and the lust of the eyes, and the pride of life, is not of the Father, but is of the world." To break "the lust of the flesh" (e.g., adultery, gluttony, drunkenness, indulgence, vanity, complacency) God sends "sickness and disease." To break "the lust of the eyes" (e.g., covetousness, worldliness, contention, strife, greed) God sends "poverty and disappointments in our relations." To break "the pride of life" (e.g., ambition, conceit, scorn, pomp) God sends "disgraces and shame."[29] God designs each of these afflictions "to reduce us to a sense and care of our duty."[30] They make us more serious and, as a result, our conscience is more "apt to work."[31] The rod is then "expounded" by the Word and "effectually applied" by the Spirit.[32]

This effectual application is manifold. First, God might be humbling us.[33] Perhaps we have been too self-conceited. If so, God "gives us to scandals that may show us what we are." Second, God might be testing us—the stability of our faith, the durability of our patience, or the sincerity of our uprightness. Third, God might be purging us.[34] Manton writes, "Reproach is like soap, which seems to defile clothes, but it cleanses them."[35]

The Manner

Manton is quick to note that God's way in affliction is always gentle.[36] He "is too strong to be resisted, too just to be questioned, and too good to be suspected."[37] That being the case, we are confident that He is not

---

28. Manton, *Psalm 119*, 7:225.
29. Manton, *Psalm 119*, 7:225.
30. Manton, *Psalm 119*, 7:226.
31. Manton, *Psalm 119*, 7:227.
32. Manton, *Psalm 119*, 7:229.
33. Manton, *Psalm 119*, 7:223. See also 8:95.
34. Manton, *Psalm 119*, 7:223. See also 8:95, 117–18.
35. Manton, *Psalm 119*, 7:223. See also 8:119.
36. Manton, *Psalm 119*, 7:28. See 1 Cor. 10:13.
37. Manton, *Exposition of James*, 29.

a passive bystander when it comes to our affliction. On the contrary, He is over it, through it, and in it, accomplishing His good purposes for us. Manton shares some very helpful insights, urging us in particular to remember four truths when we find ourselves in the furnace of affliction.

First, we must remember that God's aim in affliction is not destruction, but trial—"as gold is put into the furnace to be refined, not consumed." To put it simply, God is not trying to hurt us. Second, we must remember that we are not "in the furnace by chance, or at the will of our enemies." On the contrary, "the time is appointed, set by God." He appoints and orders all things. Third, we must remember that "God sits by the furnace...looking after his metal." He never leaves us nor forsakes us. He never abandons us to our own devices. Fourth, we must remember that God's purpose in trials is "not only to approve, but to improve; we are tried as gold, refined when tried."[38] He has a glorious purpose in view.

The Help

In seasons of suffering, we are vulnerable to a host of temptations. We are tempted to grow impatient and murmur against God.[39] We tend to think to ourselves, "There was never any so afflicted as I am."[40] We are tempted to seek revenge against "the instruments of our trouble."[41] We are tempted to despond and distrust God.[42] We are tempted to question our interest in God,[43] concluding, "I am cut off."[44] We are tempted to "atheistical thoughts, as if there were no God, no providence, no distinction between good and evil, and it were in vain to serve him."[45]

---

38. Manton, *Exposition of James*, 31.

39. Manton, *Psalm 119*, 7:375. See Jonah 4:9.

40. Manton, *Psalm 119*, 8:98.

41. Manton, *Psalm 119*, 7:375. See 2 Sam. 16:9.

42. Manton, *Psalm 119*, 7:377. See 1 Sam. 27:1.

43. Manton, *Psalm 119*, 7:377. See Judg. 6:13.

44. Manton, *Psalm 119*, 8:98. Manton adds, "We have no reason to question our adoption merely because we are put under the correction and discipline of the family." *Psalm 119*, 7:377.

45. Manton, *Psalm 119*, 7:377. See Mal. 3:14.

To overcome these temptations, we pray.[46] We look to God for all things: "When all things go well with [us], God is [our] best friend; when all things go ill with [us], God is [our] only friend."[47] He alone can help us, "either by giving support under the trouble, or removing it from us."[48] He does not always remove affliction from us, but He does always quicken, comfort, and strengthen us by His Word.[49] Through it He revives our "suffering graces" such as faith, hope, and patience, so that "we may go on cheerfully in our service."

Conclusion

"Consider mine affliction, and deliver me: for I do not forget thy law" (Ps. 119:153). In his sermon on this verse, Manton declares that we must look for affliction: "It is a vain thing to flatter ourselves with the hopes of a total exemption; many think they may be good Christians, and yet live a life of ease and peace, free from troubles and afflictions."[50] Second, we must prepare for affliction: "A well-shielded established mind in the comfort and hope of the gospel…Most Christians are not resolved, and so take to religion as a walk for recreation, not a journey, so as to be prepared for all weathers."[51] Third, we must bear affliction with patience: "Impress upon your hearts the belief of these two things—the eye of his pity, and the arm of his power."[52]

---

46. Manton states, "Till our sorrow gets a vent it rends and tears the heart." *Psalm 119*, 8:99. Again, "In deep calamities run to God, lay forth your case feelingly and with submission to the justice of his providence, trusting to his power, and submitting to his wisdom, without obtruding your model upon God, but leaving him to his own course." *Psalm 119*, 6:239.

47. Manton, *Psalm 119*, 8:99.

48. Manton, *Psalm 119*, 8:99. "After all, and in the midst of all the sufferings of God's people, their greatest desire is for more grace, the power of the quickening Spirit." Plumer, *Psalms*, 1058.

49. Manton, *Psalm 119*, 8:102. Manton states, "It is proper to the godly to love no deliverance but what God sendeth by his own means, in his own time, and to wait for it in God's way." *Psalm 119*, 9:280.

50. Manton, *Psalm 119*, 9:127. See Matt. 16:24; Luke 9:23.

51. Manton, *Psalm 119*, 9:127.

52. Manton, *Psalm 119*, 9:128, 132.

We have deep-rooted ideas of how we think God should work, but His ways rarely match our ways. The temptation is to implode emotionally. We begin to think something is wrong with God, or something is wrong with us. We begin to doubt and despair. In such times, we need to remember that deliverance from suffering comes fully and finally only in glory. To put it another way, we need to remember that the Christian life always ends well but does not always go well. In times of difficulty, we lift up our eyes to our God, reminding ourselves that He is in control. Despite changing circumstances, His love for His people does not change, and this love is the most valuable thing in life. Manton concludes, "To be chastened of God for what we have done amiss, and by that means to be reduced to the sense and practice of our duty, is one of the greatest blessings on this side heaven that can light upon us. It is an evidence of God's tender care over us, and that he will not lose us, and suffer us to perish with the unbelieving and sinful world."[53]

---

53. Manton, *Psalm 119*, 7:252.

Conclusion

"Thou art near, O LORD" (Ps. 119:151). In this declaration, the psalmist is not suggesting that God is nearer to us "in regard of his essence," for He is present in all places at all times.[1] "Whither shall I go from thy spirit? or whither shall I flee from thy presence? If I ascend up into heaven, thou art there: if I make my bed in hell, behold, thou art there" (Ps. 139:7–8). Neither is the psalmist suggesting that God is nearer to us "in regard of general providence," for He governs all things.[2] "In him we live, and move, and have our being" (Acts 17:28). What the psalmist means is that God is nearer to us in terms of His "friendly and gracious presence"—He is always ready to hear our prayers, direct us in our doubts, comfort us in our sorrows, protect us in our dangers, and deliver us in our troubles.[3] According to Manton, we enjoy this nearness because of the "saving union and communion" that exists between God and us.[4]

We are in this state of nearness to God because He has established a covenant with us, Christ has united us to Himself, and the Holy Spirit dwells within us.[5] All told, we are in a state of nearness because

---

1. Manton, *Psalm 119*, 9:102.
2. Manton, *Psalm 119*, 9:103.
3. Manton, *Psalm 119*, 9:103. See Pss. 34:18; 145:18.
4. Manton, *Psalm 119*, 9:104.
5. For John Flavel, union with Christ is "an intimate conjunction of believers to Christ, by the imparting of His Spirit to them whereby they are enabled to believe and live in Him." *Works of John Flavel*, 2:37. For Edward Pearse, "It is that spiritual conjunction or relation that is between Christ and believers, between the person of Christ and

of the mutual love that exists between God and us.[6] This is "the state of favor and reconciliation with God into which we are admitted who were before strangers and enemies."[7]

Manton makes it clear that, in addition to this state of nearness, there are "special acts of nearness." By this he means that, in terms of our experience, God is nearer to us at certain times than at others. There are occasions when we enjoy "more evidences of his favor" as He quickens, comforts, and supports us, filling our hearts "with joy and peace in believing."[8]

God brings about both the state of nearness and the special acts of nearness by means of His Word.[9] The psalmist says, "I have seen an end of all perfection: but thy commandment is exceeding broad" (Ps. 119:96). By perfection he means "beauty and strength, wit and wealth, honor and greatness."[10] He has seen an end of all these things—"an end in regard of length, duration, and continuance, and an end in regard of breadth and use."[11] Earthly perfections are good for some things, but not all things. They are unable to give "full contentment to the mind" or "full satisfaction to the heart." But God's Word, when it is applied and obeyed, provides "relief and comfort in all cases and conditions."[12] It is, says the psalmist, "exceeding broad."

God's Word is broad in its duration. Its authority continues forever: "It is an eternal rule of faith and righteousness to the church, that is more stable than heaven and earth."[13] In addition, its fruit continues

---

the person of believers, arising from His inhabitation in them by His Spirit and their closing with Him by faith." *The Best Match; or, The Soul's Espousal to Christ* (Morgan, Pa.: Soli Deo Gloria, 1994), 4.

6. Manton, *Psalm 119*, 9:106–7.

7. Manton, *Psalm 119*, 9:104.

8. Manton, *Psalm 119*, 9:105.

9. "Heart-fellowship with God is enjoyed through a love of that Word which is God's way of communing with the soul by his Holy Spirit." Spurgeon, *Golden Alphabet*, 15.

10. Manton, *Psalm 119*, 7:452.

11. Manton, *Psalm 119*, 7:452.

12. Manton, *Psalm 119*, 7:452.

13. Manton, *Psalm 119*, 7:461.

forever: "It bringeth forth the blessing of eternal life to them that keep it and obey it."[14]

God's Word is also broad in its use. Manton remarks, "A man may soon see to the bottom of the creatures, but the wisdom and purity and utility of the word of God, and the mysteries therein contained, and the spiritual estate that we have thereby, you cannot see to the end of that; it extendeth to all times, places, persons, actions, and circumstances of actions; it hath an inconceivable vastness of purity and spirituality."[15] In God's Word, we discover "remedies for every malady" and "storehouses for every comfort." We find all that is necessary for our holiness and happiness.[16]

Given the sufficiency of God's Word to bring us near to God, we busy ourselves with it. We seek Him in His Word, and certainly not apart from it or in contradiction to it.[17] For Manton, this pursuit is summed up in three related acts: meditating, delighting, and obeying, for "meditation breedeth delight, and delight helpeth memory and practice."[18] As we devote ourselves to God's Word (in meditating, delighting, and obeying), He impresses His excellencies on us, thereby stirring our faith, hope, and love whereby we make suitable returns to Him in prayer and praise. Manton summarizes as follows:

> Christianity, as it is acted by us, is but the exercise of faith, hope, and love. Now, the eternal fruition of God is the matter that all these graces are conversant about. Faith believeth that there is an eternal being, and that our happiness lieth in the fruition of him (Hebrews 11:6). Love is that which levelleth and directeth all our actions to this blessed end, that we may see God and enjoy him as our portion and felicity (Psalm 73:25). Our desires are after him, our delights in him; it is our work to please him, our happiness to enjoy him. The truth of his eternal being is the object of our

---

14. Manton, *Psalm 119*, 7:461.

15. Manton, *Psalm 119*, 7:459.

16. Manton, *Psalm 119*, 7:459–60.

17. "Let us beware of that fanaticism which is guided by impulses and despises the written Word." Plumer, *Psalms*, 1032.

18. Manton, *Psalm 119*, 6:146.

hope; so the apprehension of him as our chief good and felicity
is the object of our love, so as he is capable of being enjoyed; and
our participated eternity is the object of our faith: this is the end
of all our desires and labors, and the expectation of this fortifieth
us against all the difficulties of our pilgrimage, and so directeth us
what to mind, be, and do (2 Corinthians 5:9).[19]

This emphasis is how Manton understands the blessed man's pursuit in Psalm 119. At the foundation stands the conviction that as we
love and obey God's Word, the blessed God communes with us by His
Spirit, conveying sweet influences on our soul through His Word.[20]
Thus, we expect God to speak to us—not subjectively through inner
urgings but objectively through His Word.[21] Manton's spirituality of
the Word is a timely remedy for the subjective mysticism that enthralls
much of modern evangelicalism. It is a reminder that the Bible is God's
voice—that which "goeth forth" out of God's mouth (Isa. 55:11). It is
as powerful as the rain and snow that "cometh down…from heaven,
and returneth not thither, but watereth the earth, and maketh it bring
forth and bud, that it may give seed to the sower, and bread to the
eater" (Isa. 55:10). For this reason, we listen to the Bible as if we heard
God speaking to us from heaven, rejoicing as those who find "great
spoil" (Ps. 119:162).

---

19. Manton, *Psalm 119*, 7:398–99.

20. "The Bible does not so much need a comment, as the soul does the light of the
Holy Spirit." Plumer, *Psalms*, 1031.

21. This emphasis is not confined to Manton's exposition of Psalm 119 but occu-
pies a significant place throughout his collected sermons. See Manton, *Works*, 1:93–97,
272–73; 3:64; 4:114–78; 5:481–82, 487–500; 9:335–36, 345–46; 10:110, 201, 221,
227–40; 11:21–23; 12:293, 319–21; 15:154–74, 385–87; 16:294; 17:126–35, 353–63;
18:16, 20, 25–26.

Rules for Meditation

1. Whatever you meditate upon must be drawn down to application (Job 5:27).... All the while we stay in generals we do but bend the bow; when we come to application we let fly the arrow, and we hit the mark when we come to return upon our own souls.

2. Do not pry further than God hath revealed; your thoughts must be still bounded by the word. There is no duty that a fanatic brain is more apt to abuse than meditation.... To pry into the mysteries of divine decrees were to disturb affection, not to raise it; nice disputes feed curiosity, not religion.

3. When you meditate of God you must do it with great care and reverence; his perfections are matter rather of admiration than inquiry.... God is said to dwell in light to show his majesty, and to dwell in darkness to show his incomprehensibleness. Do not entangle yourselves while you are about to raise your zeal; the full knowledge of these things is our portion in heaven.

4. In meditating on common things, keep in mind a spiritual purpose.... Philosophers study the creatures to find out their natural causes, we to find our arguments of worship and religion.

The twelve rules for meditation are from Manton, *Sermons on Genesis 24:63,* 17:277–81.

5. Take heed of creating a snare to your souls. Some sins are catching, like fire in straw, and we cannot think of them without infection and temptation; the very thoughts may beget a sudden delight and tickling, which may pass through us like lightning and set us all on fire.

6. Meditate of those things especially which you have most need of.... Seasonable thoughts have the greatest influence.

7. Whatever you meditate upon, take heed of slightness. Transient thoughts leave no impression.... A skipping mind, that wandereth from one meditation to another, seldom profiteth.... There is a folly in man, when once we apprehend a thing; curiosity being satisfied, we begin to loath it, the first apprehension having as it were deflowered it, but at last they lose their power and virtue.... A glance doth not discover the worth of anything.

8. Come not off from holy thoughts till you find profit by them, either sweet tastes and relishes of the love of God, or high affections kindled towards God, or strong resolutions begotten in yourselves.... We cannot always expect raptures and high elevations; it is some fruit if it maketh you fall to prayer and holy complaints.

9. Be thankful to God when he blesseth you in meditation, or else you will find difficulty in the next.

10. Do not bridle up the free spirit by rules of method. That which God calleth for is religion, not logic.... Voluntary and free meditations are most smart and pregnant.

11. Your success in the duty is not to be measured by the multitude and subtlety of the thoughts, but the sincerity of them.

12. You must begin and end all with prayer. Duties are subservient one to another. In the beginning you must pray for a blessing upon the duty, and in the end commend your souls and resolutions to God.

Contemplation

Contemplation figures prominently in medieval spirituality, which conceives of the spiritual life not as growing in the knowledge of God but rather as removing all affirmations concerning God until we arrive at silence—the bare communion of the soul with God. The goal is to reach union with God—a point where the Creator/creature distinction is no longer perceived. Key to this is the contemplation of the spiritual, the celestial, the beautiful, or the divine. Although Manton acknowledges the possibility of such an experience, he is unwilling to embrace it as normative. He writes,

> The schoolmen and other writers of devotion usually distinguish between consideration, meditation, and contemplation. Consideration is a thinking of truth, and a rolling of it in the understanding and memory. Meditation is an enforcing of truth upon the soul by discourse of variety of pressing arguments. Contemplation is the fruit and perfection of meditation; and this they make a supernatural elevation of the mind, by which it adhereth to God, and pauseth in the sight of God and glory without any variety of discourse; the soul being dazzled with the majesty of God, or the glory of heaven, and transported into a present joy, the use of reason is for a time suspended, and the soul is cast into a kind of sleep and quietness of intuition, staring and gazing with ravishing sweetness upon the divine excellences and glory of our hopes. In short, contemplation is a ravishing sight without

discourse, the work of reason not discoursing, but raised and ecstasied into the highest way of apprehension.[1]

Manton believes that contemplation (i.e., "a supernatural elevation of the mind") is described in Acts 10:10, 2 Corinthians 12:2, and Revelation 1:10. He is not convinced, however, that we should expect such experiences today.[2] God does occasionally grant a measure of the beatific vision in the present,[3] which results in "strong pangs and ecstasies of love, which for a while do suspend and forbid the distinct use of reason, and cast the soul into a quiet silent gaze."[4] We consider Christ's "beauty and perfection" as revealed in Scripture. As we dwell on Him with "religious thoughts," our love grows stronger. When our love is "heightened unto the utmost degree," it "shutteth the eyes of our souls," and we please ourselves "in a more intimate feeling."[5] In this condition, "the soul falleth into the arms of Christ, and claspeth about Christ with the arms of its own love."

For Manton, this "rapturous" experience is depicted in the Song of Solomon.[6] "That whole song," says he, "concerneth our communion with Christ in heaven and in the ordinances."[7] Concerning Song of

---

1. Manton, *Sermons on Genesis 24:63*, 17:293.

2. Manton, *Sermons on Genesis 24:63*, 17:294.

3. John Owen writes, "The enjoyment of God by sight, is commonly called the beatific vision, and, it is the sole fountain of all the actings of our souls in the state of blessedness." *The Glorious Mystery of the Person of Christ, God and Man: To Which Are Subjoined, Meditations and Discourses on the Glory of Christ* (New York: Robert Carter, 1839), 383. For an analysis of the Puritan focus on the Beatific Vision, see Joel R. Beeke and Mark Jones, *A Puritan Theology* (Grand Rapids: Reformation Heritage Books, 2012), 824–25.

4. Manton, *Sermons on Genesis 24:63*, 17:294.

5. Manton, *Sermons on Genesis 24:63*, 17:294–95.

6. Manton writes, "In the Book of Canticles communion with Christ is set forth by banquets and marriages, and spiritual things are shadowed out by corporal fairness and sweetness." *Sermons on Genesis 24:63*, 17:304. He inherits this view from Bernard of Clairvaux. *Sermons on Genesis 24:63*, 17:301. For a concise study of Bernard's spirituality of mystical union, as derived from the Song of Songs, see Arie de Reuver, *Sweet Communion: Trajectories of Spirituality from the Middle Ages through the Further Reformation*, trans. James A. De Jong (Grand Rapids: Baker Academic, 2007), 27–63.

7. Manton, *Sermons on Genesis 24:63*, 17:295. John Owen summarizes his understanding of the Song as follows: "Then may a man judge himself to have somewhat

Solomon 7:8 in particular, he writes, "The palm-tree hath a long naked bark, and carrieth all its leaves, branches and fruits upwards; it noteth the religious ascent of the soul in spiritual exercises, when the thoughts do not run out in underwood and lower branches, in earthly thoughts and carnal distractions. Well, then, in the top of the palm-tree there we taste the sweetness of Christ, and the soul is ravished and spiritually made drunk with the clusters of his grapes."[8]

Manton is careful to acknowledge that we cannot produce these raptures, nor should we pursue them. We are not even to pray for them. Rather, "God gives them when he seeth fit."[9] For our part, we are to "content ourselves with grace, and peace, and joy in the Holy Ghost."[10]

---

profited in the experience of a mystery of a blessed intercourse and communion with Christ, when the expressions of love in that holy Dialogue, the Song, do give light and life unto his mind, and efficaciously communicate unto him an experience of their power. But because these things are little understood by many, the book itself is much neglected, if not despised." John Owen, *Christologia; or, a Declaration of the Glorious Mystery of the Person of Christ, God and Man* (Glasgow: Ebenezer Miller, 1790), 95. See also John Owen, *Meditations and Discourses on the Glory of Christ in Two Parts* (Edinburgh: William Gray, 1750), 115.

8. Manton, *Sermons on Genesis 24:63*, 17:295–96.

9. These raptures are not duties to be pursued but experiences to be enjoyed. "Many times Christians oppress their souls by their indiscreet aims." We need to be very careful with these experiences because we easily delude ourselves. We know the difference by the result. "Experiences from God enlarge our hearts for service, and make us more humble, as the highest flames tremble most." Manton, *Sermons on Genesis 24:63*, 17:296.

10. Manton, *Sermons on Genesis 24:63*, 17:297.

Bibliography

Aristotle. *Nicomachean Ethics*. In *The Works of Aristotle*. Vol 9. Edited by W. D. Ross. Oxford: Oxford University Press, 1963.

Augustine. *A Select Library of the Nicene and Post-Nicene Fathers of the Christian Church*. Vol. 2, *The City of God*. Edited by P. Schaff. New York: Random House, 1948.

Bates, William. "A Funeral Sermon Preached upon the Death of the Reverend and Excellent Divine, Dr. Thomas Manton." In Manton, *Works*.

Baxter, Richard. *The Practical Works of Richard Baxter: Select Treatises*. London: Blackie & Son, 1863. Reprint, Grand Rapids: Baker, 1981.

Bayly, Lewis. *The Practice of Piety: Directing a Christian How to Walk, That He May Please God*. 1613. Reprint, Morgan, Pa.: Soli Deo Gloria, 2003.

Beeke, Joel R. "The Lasting Power of Reformed Experiential Preaching." In *Puritan Reformed Spirituality*. Grand Rapids: Reformation Heritage Books, 2004.

Beeke, Joel R., and Mark Jones. *A Puritan Theology*. Grand Rapids: Reformation Heritage Books, 2012.

Beeke, Joel R., and Randall J. Pederson. *Meet the Puritans: With a Guide to Modern Reprints*. Grand Rapids: Reformation Heritage Books, 2006.

Blench, J. W. *Preaching in England in the Late Fifteenth and Sixteenth Centuries*. New York: Barnes & Noble, 1964.

Bolton, Robert. *A Discourse about the State of True Happiness: Delivered in Certain Sermons in Oxford, and at Paul's Cross.* London, 1611.

Breward, Ian. "William Perkins and the Origins of Puritan Casuistry." *The Evangelist Quarterly* 40 (1968): 16–22.

Bridges, Charles. *Psalm 119: An Exposition.* 1827. Reprint, Edinburgh: Banner of Truth, 1974.

Bunyan, John. *The Greatness of the Soul, and Unspeakableness of the Loss Thereof, &c.* In *The Miscellaneous Works of John Bunyan.* Oxford: Clarendon Press, 1981.

———. *A Treatise on the Fear of God.* 1679. Reprint, Morgan, Pa.: Soli Deo Gloria, 1999.

Calamy, Edmund. *An Abridgement of Mr. Baxter's History of His Life and Times.* London, 1702.

———. *The Nonconformist's Memorial: Being an Account of the Ministers, Who Were Ejected or Silenced after the Restoration, Particularly by the Act of Uniformity, Which Took Place on Bartholomew-Day, Aug. 24, 1662.* London, 1775.

Calvin, John. *Calvin's Commentaries.* Vol. 19, *Commentaries on the Epistle of the Apostle Paul to the Romans.* Grand Rapids: Baker Books, 2003.

———. *Calvin's Commentaries.* Vol. 6, *Commentary on the Book of Psalms.* Translated by James Anderson. Grand Rapids: Baker Books, 2003.

———. *Institutes of the Christian Religion.* In *The Library of Christian Classics.* Vols. 20–21. Edited by J. T. McNeill. Philadelphia: Westminster Press, 1960.

———. *Sermons on the Beatitudes.* Translated by Robert White. 1562. Reprint, Edinburgh: Banner of Truth, 2006.

Charnock, Stephen. *Discourses upon the Existence and Attributes of God.* 1853. Reprint, Grand Rapids: Baker, 1990.

Clarkson, David. *The Works of David Clarkson.* 3 vols. 1864–1865. Reprint, Edinburgh: Banner of Truth, 1988.

Cooper, Derek. "The Ecumenical Exegete: Thomas Manton's Commentary on James in Relation to Its Protestant Predecessors, Contemporaries and Successors." PhD thesis, Lutheran Theological Seminary, 2008.

———. *Thomas Manton: A Guided Tour of the Life and Thought of a Puritan Pastor*. Phillipsburg, N.J.: P&R Publishing, 2011.

Davies, Horton. *Worship and Theology in England from Andrewes to Baxter and Fox, 1603–1690*. Princeton, N.J.: Princeton University Press, 1975.

———. *The Worship of English Puritans*. Morgan, Pa.: Soli Deo Gloria, 1997.

de Reuver, Arie. *Sweet Communion: Trajectories of Spirituality from the Middle Ages through the Further Reformation*. Translated by James A. De Jong. Grand Rapids: Baker Academic, 2007.

Dolezal, James E. *All That Is in God: Evangelical Theology and the Challenge of Classical Christian Theism*. Grand Rapids: Reformation Heritage Books, 2017.

Edwards, Jonathan. *Charity and Its Fruits: Christian Love as Manifested in the Heart and Life*. 1852. Reprint, Edinburgh: Banner of Truth, 2000.

———. *On Religious Affections*. In *The Works of Jonathan Edwards*. 2 vols. 1834. Reprint, Peabody, Mass.: Hendrickson, 1998.

Flavel, John. *The Works of John Flavel*. London: W. Baynes and Son, 1820. Reprint, London: Banner of Truth, 1968.

George, Timothy. Introduction to *For All the Saints: Evangelical Theology and Christian Spirituality*. Edited by Timothy George and Alister McGrath. Louisville, Ky.: Westminster John Knox, 2003.

Gouge, William. *Of Domesticall Duties: Eight Treatises*. London, 1622.

Greaves, Richard. "The Puritan-Nonconformist Tradition in England, 1560–1700: Historiographical Reflections." *Albion* 17 (1985): 449–86.

Gribben, Crawford. "Thomas Manton and the Spirituality of Solitude." *Eusebeia: The Bulletin of the Jonathan Edwards Centre for Reformed Spirituality* 6 (Spring 2007): 21–23.

Gurnall, William. *The Christian in Complete Armor: A Treatise of the Saints' War against the Devil.* 1662–1665. Reprint, Edinburgh: Banner of Truth, 1995.

Harris, Robert. *The Way of True Happiness, Delivered in Twenty-Four Sermons upon the Beatitudes.* 1653. Reprint, Morgan, Pa.: Soli Deo Gloria, 1998.

Harris, William. "Some Memoirs of the Life and Character of the Reverend and Learned Thomas Manton, D. D." In Manton, *Works*.

Henry, Matthew. *Commentary on the Whole Bible.* Edited by Leslie F. Church. Grand Rapids: Zondervan, 1961.

Hinson, E. Glenn. "Puritan Spirituality." In *Protestant Spiritual Traditions*. Edited by F. C. Senn. New York: Paulist Press, 1986.

Hunt, Arnold. *The Art of Hearing: English Preachers and Their Audiences, 1590–1640.* Cambridge: Cambridge University Press, 2010.

James, William. *The Varieties of Religious Experience.* London: Collins, 1960.

Jones, Hywel. *Psalm 119 for Life: Living Today in the Light of the Word.* Faverdale North, UK: EP Books, 2009.

Keeble, Neil. "Puritan Spirituality." In *The Westminster Dictionary of Christian Spirituality*. Edited by G. S. Wakefield. Philadelphia: Westminster Press, 1983.

Kuivenhoven, Maarten. "Condemning Coldness and Sleepy Dullness: The Concept of Urgency in the Preaching Models of Richard Baxter and William Perkins." *Puritan Reformed Journal* 4, no. 2 (July 2012): 180–200.

Louth, Andrew. *The Origins of the Christian Mystical Tradition from Plato to Denys.* Oxford: Clarendon Press, 1981.

Lovelace, Richard. *Dynamics of Spiritual Life: An Evangelical Theology of Renewal.* Downers Grove, Ill.: IVP Academic, 1979.

MacLean, Donald J. "Thomas Manton (1620–1677)." In *James Durham (1622–1658) and the Gospel Offer in Its Seventeenth-Century Context.* Göttingen: Vandenhoeck & Ruprecht, 2015.

Manton, Thomas. *The Complete Works of Thomas Manton.* 22 vols. London: James Nisbet, 1870–1875. Reprint, Birmingham, Ala.: Solid Ground Christian Books, 2008.

McKim, Donald Keith. *Ramism in William Perkins's Theology.* New York: Peter Lang, 1987.

M'Gavin, William. "Life of John Knox." In John Knox, *The History of the Reformation of Religion in Scotland.* Glasgow: Blackie, Fullarton, & Co., 1831.

Miller, Perry. *The New England Mind.* New York: Macmillan, 1939.

Morrissey, Mary. "Scripture, Style, and Persuasion in Seventeenth-Century English Theories of Preaching." *Journal of Ecclesiastical History* 53, no. 4 (October 2002): 686–706.

Mosse, George L. *The Holy Pretence: A Study in Christianity and Reason of State from William Perkins to John Winthrop.* Oxford: Blackwell, 1957.

Muller, Richard. "William Perkins and the Protestant Exegetical Tradition: Interpretation, Style and Method." In *A Commentary on Hebrews 11 (1609 Edition).* Edited by John H. Augustine. New York: Pilgrim Press, 1991.

Murray, John. "The Guidance of the Holy Spirit." In Sinclair B. Ferguson, *From the Mouth of God: Trusting, Reading, and Applying the Bible.* Edinburgh: Banner of Truth, 2014.

Nee, Watchman. *The Release of the Spirit.* Bombay: Gospel Literature Service, 1965.

Old, Hughes Oliphant. *The Reading and Preaching of the Scriptures in the Worship of the Christian Church.* 7 vols. Grand Rapids: Eerdmans, 2002.

Owen, John. *Christologia; or, a Declaration of the Glorious Mystery of the Person of Christ, God and Man.* Glasgow: Ebenezer Miller, 1790.

————. *The Glorious Mystery of the Person of Christ, God and Man: To Which Are Subjoined, Meditations and Discourses on the Glory of Christ.* New York: Robert Carter, 1839.

————. *Meditations and Discourses on the Glory of Christ in Two Parts.* Edinburgh: William Gray, 1750.

————. *The Works of John Owen.* Edited by William H. Goold. 1850–1853. Reprint, Edinburgh: Banner of Truth, 1974.

Packer, J. I. *A Quest for Godliness: The Puritan Vision of the Christian Life.* Wheaton, Ill.: Crossway, 1990.

Packer, J. I., and Carolyn Nystrom. *Guard Us, Guide Us: Divine Leading in Life's Decisions.* Grand Rapids: Baker Books, 2008.

Pearse, Edward. *The Best Match; or, The Soul's Espousal to Christ.* Morgan, Pa.: Soli Deo Gloria, 1994.

Penington, Isaac. *Letters of Isaac Penington.* 2nd ed. London: Holdsworth and Ball, 1829.

Perkins, William. *A Faithful and Plain Exposition upon the Two First Verses of the Second Chapter of Zephaniah.* In *Works of William Perkins.* London, 1631.

————. *A Godly and Learned Exposition upon Christ's Sermon in the Mount.* In *Works of William Perkins.* London, 1631.

————. *A Godly and Learned Exposition upon the Whole Epistle of Jude.* London: Felix Kingston, 1606.

————. *A Reformed Catholic; or, A Declaration Showing How Near We May Come to the Present Church of Rome in Sundry Points of Religion, and Wherein We Must Forever Depart from Them.* In *Works of William Perkins.* London, 1608.

————. *A Treatise Tending unto a Declaration, Whether a Man Be in the Estate of Damnation, or in the Estate of Grace: and if He Be in the First, How He May in Time Come out of It: if in the Second, How He May Discern It, and Persevere in the Same to the End.* In *Works of William Perkins.* London, 1608.

————. *The Whole Treatise of the Cases of Conscience, Distinguished into Three Books.* London, 1632.

————. *The Works of William Perkins.* 3 vols. London, 1608, 1631.

————. *The Works of William Perkins.* Vol. 2, *The Art of Prophesying; or, A Treatise concerning the Sacred and Only True Manner and Method of Preaching.* London, 1631.

Pipa, Joseph A. "William Perkins and the Development of Puritan Preaching." Unpublished PhD diss., Westminster Theological Seminary, 1985.

Plumer, William. *Psalms: A Critical and Expository Commentary with Doctrinal and Practical Remarks.* 1867. Reprint, Edinburgh: Banner of Truth, 1975.

Richardson, Adam. "Thomas Manton and the Presbyterians in Interregnum and Restoration England." PhD thesis, University of Leicester, 2014.

Ryle, J. C. "An Estimate of Manton." In Manton, *Works.*

Scaramelli, G. B. *A Handbook of Mystical Theology.* Translated by D. H. S. Nicholson. 1913. Reprint, Berwick, Maine: Ibis Press, 2005.

Shepard, Thomas. *The Sincere Convert: Discovering the Small Number of True Believers and the Great Difficulty of Saving Conversion.* In *The Sincere Convert and the Sound Believer.* Boston: Doctrinal Tract and Book Society, 1853. Reprint, Morgan, Pa.: Soli Deo Gloria, 1999.

Spurgeon, Charles. *The Golden Alphabet: A Devotional Commentary on Psalm 119.* Pasadena, Tex.: Pilgrim Publications, 1969.

Swinnock, George. *The Works of George Swinnock.* 5 vols. Edinburgh: James Nichol, 1868. Reprint, London: Banner of Truth, 1992.

Talbot, Mark. "Growing in the Grace and Knowledge of Our Lord and Savior Jesus Christ." In *For All the Saints: Evangelical Theology and Christian Spirituality.* Edited by Timothy George and Alister McGrath. Louisville, Ky.: Westminster John Knox, 2003.

Toon, Peter. *From Mind to Heart: Christian Meditation Today.* Grand Rapids: Baker, 1987.

Warfield, B. B. *The Works of Benjamin Warfield.* Vol. 6, *The Westminster Assembly and Its Work.* Grand Rapids: Baker Books, 2003.

Watson, Thomas. *All Things of Good; or, A Divine Cordial.* 1663. Reprint, Edinburgh: Banner of Truth, 1994.

———. *The Beatitudes: An Exposition of Matthew 5:1–12.* 1660. Reprint, Edinburgh: Banner of Truth, 1994.

Wilson, Thomas. *David's Zeal for Zion: A Sermon Preached before the Honourable House of Commons, April 4, 1641.* London, 1641.

Wood, Anthony. *Athenae Oxonienses.* 2 vols. London, 1691.

Yuille, J. Stephen. "The Boundless and Blessed God: The Legacy of Amandus Polanus in the Theology of George Swinnock." In *Learning from the Past: Essays on Reception, Catholicity and Dialogue in Honor of Anthony N. S. Lane.* Edited by Jon Balserak and Richard Snoddy. London: T&T Clark, 2015.

———. "Conversing with God's Word: Scripture Meditation in the Piety of George Swinnock." *Journal of Spiritual Formation and Soul Care* 5 (2012): 35–55.

———. *The Inner Sanctum of Puritan Piety: John Flavel's Doctrine of Mystical Union with Christ.* Grand Rapids: Reformation Heritage Books, 2007.

———. *Puritan Spirituality: The Fear of God in the Affective Theology of George Swinnock.* Milton Keynes, UK: Paternoster, 2007.

———. "A Simple Method: William Perkins and the Shaping of the Protestant Pulpit." *Puritan Reformed Journal* 9, no. 1 (January 2017): 215–30.